THE AI LEADERSHIP ACCELERATOR

"Multiplying Your Impact Through Strategic AI Partnership"

MAJOR F. RIDDICK, JR.

publish your dreams

The information provided in this book is designed to provide helpful information on the subjects discussed. This book is not meant to be used, nor should it be used, to diagnose or treat any medical condition. For diagnosis or treatment of any medical problem, consult your own physician. The publisher and author are not responsible for any specific outcomes, health or otherwise, that may result from applying the methods suggested in this book.

First Edition

Published 2026

ISBN:

E-Book: 978-1-966418-42-9

Paperback: 978-1-966418-43-6

Hardcover: 978-1-966418-44-3

Cover design by AI Gemini and Major F. Riddick, Jr.

Interior design by Claude.ai

For more information:

Strategic Solutions Center

www.strategicsolutionscenter.com

mriddick@strategicsolutionscenter.com.

Printed in USA

ACKNOWLEDGEMENTS

No book is truly the work of one person. While my name is on the cover, these pages were shaped by a lifetime of conversations, high-stakes challenges, and the people who invested in me long before a manuscript existed.

To the friends and colleagues who nudged, prodded, and outright challenged me for years to "write it down" thank you for your persistence. You saw patterns in my journey that I hadn't yet recognized, and you reminded me that experience only carries its full value when it is shared.

I am deeply grateful to Governor Parris Glendening. He provided the opportunities that stretched me and the trust that allowed me to grow into higher levels of responsibility. The lessons I learned under his leadership at the county and state levels remain the bedrock of how I serve today.

To my parents, Viola C. Riddick and Major F. Riddick, Sr., thank you for the grounding that lasts a lifetime. You taught me how to work when no one is watching and how to pursue excellence without ever losing my humanity. Whatever impact this book has, it started with what you poured into me.

To my wife, Manervia, and my daughter, Myrica: writing a book is an endurance sport. You provided the encouragement and the space I needed when the finish line felt far away. Your love is the reason I know leadership matters in the first place.

I also want to recognize the countless public officials and professionals I've served alongside. Leadership is never a solo act; it's a team effort across agencies and communities. To those of you now leading at the highest levels, I am honored to have been part of your journey.

A special thank you to Kane and Alessia Minkus of Industry Rockstar. Your training and discipline reinforced a vital truth: learning isn't an event, it's a practice. You helped me stay sharp and relevant in an evolving, AI-driven world.

Finally, I want to acknowledge my "thinking partners," to pressure-test ideas and refine my perspectives was a living exercise in the book's core theme: that the future belongs to leaders who combine human wisdom with intelligent assistance.

To everyone who opened a door, offered a critique, or simply believed this book needed to exist: thank you. The value in these pages is the fruit of your investment.

TABLE OF CONTENTS

PREFACE

The world did not ask for permission to change, but here we are.

For four decades, I have stood in the middle of that change. I have led teams through high-stakes assignments, navigated the quiet weight of public service, and learned, often through the bruising reality of struggle, what it truly takes to move people toward a common goal. For years, colleagues and friends have asked me when I would finally put these lessons on paper. I carried their encouragement from one challenge to the next until the timing finally felt right.

That time is now.

I am writing this because we are at a unique crossroads. Leadership has always required four pillars: character, competence, communication, and courage. But today, a fifth element has entered the room. Artificial intelligence is no longer a futuristic concept; it is actively reshaping how we decide, work, and compete.

The opportunity before you is not merely to become more technical. The opportunity is to become more effective. This book is the bridge between timeless leadership principles and the modern tools that multiply your impact.

The Human at the Center

Over forty years of leadership, I have learned one simple, unshakeable truth: leadership is about people. It is about coaching others to exceed what they once thought possible. While a title might open a door, it is trust and preparation that inspire people to walk through it.

Because of this, I want to be very clear about what AI is and what it is not. AI cannot replace your values. It cannot substitute for your judgment or your heart. It is, however, a powerful force multiplier. It can analyze data in seconds, simulate complex scenarios, and remove the friction from your daily execution. Used wisely, AI frees you to do the work that only you can do: coaching, inspiring, and serving.

How to Use This Accelerator

This is not a book of theory. It is an accelerator designed for immediate action. Whether you are leading a small team or an entire organization, I want you to approach these pages as a builder.

- Practice in small steps. Choose one action item per chapter and apply it within the week. Momentum is a leader's best friend.
- Accelerate, don't outsource. Use AI to support your thinking but always apply your own experience to the final decision.
- Lead in community. Share these frameworks with your team. Use them in your workshops and strategic planning. Leadership grows fastest when it is shared.

A Call to Service

At my core, I believe leadership is service. It is the act of putting others first and helping talent rise, even when it is inconvenient. That principle is woven into every page of this book because it is the only kind of leadership that endures.

Thank you for choosing to invest in your growth. If you apply what you learn here with humility and consistency, you will do more than just improve your performance. You will expand your influence and increase the positive impact you make on the world.

The future of leadership is here. Let's begin.

Introduction

The AI Leadership Accelerator

Training Tools for the Next Generation

As a kid, I spent countless hours throwing rocks at telephone poles from long distances. Some days, most throws would miss their mark. But I didn't give up. Over time, my accuracy improved dramatically. When my friends watched me hit the poles with increasing frequency, it would bring smiles and amazement.

They often wondered: How did I develop this skill? Was it a gift for a select few, or something everyone could learn and develop? In many ways, leadership and confidence work the same way and we wish someone would teach us the secret.

Some leaders throw the rock too hard, overconfident that it will hit the pole. But it sails past and misses the target. Then there are leaders who throw too softly, without enough momentum to reach the pole or stay on course. They're too tentative, unsure of their approach, so the rock never hits its mark.

The fundamental question is: *How can I throw the rock so that it consistently hits the pole?*

Isn't that what we as leaders are always asking? How far can our vision reach? How many people can we impact? How well will our teams develop? How many professionals can we transform?

Leadership Is Not a One-Time Event

Leadership is a fluid process with constantly changing conditions. Sometimes things flow smoothly. Sometimes you throw a little too hard and miss the target. Confidence fluctuates impacted by personal performance, the size of assignments, belief in oneself, support from others, mistakes made, and the trust you've built.

Questioning one's confidence is a practical and common experience. Understanding who you are, how you're seen by others, and what you were designed to do is foundational for leadership confidence and ultimately, for leadership effectiveness.

Here's what I discovered over four decades of leadership: there is a direct connection between competence and confidence. However, you can be competent and still not confident. And you can be confident and still not competent. Both must work together. A confident leader understands the critical importance of adaptability in an environment where change is the only constant.

Leading in the Age of AI

Today's leaders face a unique challenge and opportunity. The digital transformation, particularly the emergence of artificial intelligence isn't just changing *what* we do; it's transforming *how* we think, operate, and lead.

AI is not here to replace leadership, it's here to multiply your impact. The leaders who will thrive in the coming decades are those who master the integration of timeless leadership principles with cutting-edge tools. They understand that technology enhances human capability; it doesn't diminish the need for authentic, values-driven leadership.

This book bridges that gap. It combines proven frameworks from leadership masters like Stephen Covey, John Maxwell, Les Brown, Tony Robbins, and T.D. Jakes with practical AI applications that will accelerate your leadership development and amplify your effectiveness.

Lessons from the Field

Over my career in public service, government, real estate, technology consulting, and airport concessions, I've learned that leadership comes down to one fundamental truth: it's about making others feel important while coaching them to exceed their own expectations.

Many of my former team members still say, "Once you've worked for Major, you always work for Major." They say it with fondness not because I was the boss, but because I invested in them. I modeled Covey's 7 Habits. I embraced Maxwell's principle of transitioning from boss to leader. I focused on getting people to follow willingly, not through rank or authority.

One defining moment came during a budget season when I served as Director of the Office of Management and Budget. We faced an impossible deadline the final document had to be picked up by the county printer over the weekend for Monday morning delivery to officials and the press.

Several staff members didn't believe we could finish in time. It was an emotional, high-stakes moment. My deputy and two other staff members stayed for 37 straight hours. I sent others home to rest after acknowledging their contributions. We battled technology failures, copier breakdowns, and organizational challenges.

Those who went home returned the next morning with breakfast for the team. The energy was electric. I was the only one who truly believed we would make it but they kept working anyway. We finished on time.

The pride they felt afterward was extraordinary. That's the essence of leadership: inspiring people to achieve what they thought was impossible not through force, but through belief, support, and genuine care.

What This Book Will Do for You

This book is designed as an *accelerator* a tool to multiply your leadership impact through condensed learning and practical application. Whether you're a mid-level manager preparing for executive leadership, a new executive finding your footing, a young entrepreneur building your first team, or a government leader transitioning sectors, this book meets you where you are.

Throughout these pages, you will:

- Master the fundamentals of transformational leadership grounded in proven frameworks
- Develop authentic confidence by understanding who you are and how you're perceived
- Learn to communicate effectively with your team to drive high performance and adaptability
- Build self-awareness and contextual understanding the twin pillars of effective leadership

- Discover how AI tools can enhance your decision-making, strategy, and team development
- Apply practical exercises, reflection questions, and AI-powered tools in each chapter

Each chapter is structured with actionable frameworks, real-world examples from decades of leadership experience, and dedicated sections on AI applications. You'll find exercises to implement immediately and reflection questions to deepen your understanding.

The goal isn't just knowledge it's transformation. This book is about becoming the kind of leader people choose to follow, the kind who develops others into their best selves, and the kind who leverages every available tool including AI to create sustainable impact.

Why AI Matters for Leaders

Some leaders view AI with skepticism or fear. I see it differently. Throughout my career, I've witnessed how the right tools from budget software to project management systems can free leaders to focus on what truly matters: people, strategy, and vision.

AI is the next evolution of those tools. It can analyze data faster, identify patterns you might miss, draft communications, simulate scenarios, and provide insights that enhance not replace your judgment. Used wisely, AI becomes your force multiplier.

This book doesn't just tell you AI is important it shows you exactly how to integrate it into your leadership practice. Each chapter includes dedicated AI sections with specific tools, prompts, and applications you can use immediately.

Your Journey Starts Here

One of the most surprising insights from my 40+ years in leadership is this: I only applied for my first job in government. Every position after that was offered to me. Why? Because I consistently delivered on assignments, discovered needs before my supervisors recognized them, and built a reputation for excellence and reliability.

That's the power of effective leadership combined with strategic thinking. When you develop these capabilities and leverage AI to amplify them opportunities find you.

Navigating the journey of competence with confidence can foster creativity and collaboration, especially in environments where AI consulting assists with operational transformation. This book serves as both beacon and transformative force guiding you through a leadership and digital path toward sustainable growth and lasting impact.

Let's begin the journey together.

Major F. Riddick, Jr.

PART 1

LEADING YOURSELF FIRST

- *Chapter 1: Building Authentic Confidence*
- *Chapter 2: Self-Awareness and Leadership Identity*
- *Chapter 3: Communication for High Performance*
- *Chapter 4: Adaptability in Changing Environments*

CHAPTER 1

BUILDING AUTHENTIC CONFIDENCE

Building Authentic Confidence

"You don't have to be great to get started,

but you have to get started to be great."

Les Brown

The Rock and the Pole

I spent countless childhood hours perfecting one seemingly simple skill: throwing rocks at telephone poles from increasingly greater distances. On some days, I'd miss more often than I'd hit. The rock would sail wide left, fall short, or veer off course. Frustration would creep in.

But I kept throwing.

Over time, something shifted. My accuracy improved. I could feel the weight of the rock differently, judge the distance more precisely, adjust for wind and angle instinctively. When my friends watched me hit pole after pole with growing consistency, they were amazed. They asked the question that would eventually shape my understanding of leadership:

"How do you do that? Were you just born with it?"

The truth is, I wasn't born with perfect aim. I developed it through practice, failure, adjustment, and persistence. The confidence to throw from greater distances came *after* building competence, not before.

Leadership confidence works the same way. It's not a gift bestowed on a select few. It's a skill developed through deliberate practice, honest self-assessment, and the courage to keep throwing even when you miss the mark.

The Confidence-Competence Connection

One of the most persistent myths in leadership development is that confidence must precede action. We tell ourselves, "I'll step up when I feel more confident," or "I'll take that role when I'm ready." But this thinking has it backward.

Here's what I've learned over four decades of leadership: Confidence is both a prerequisite and a result of competence. They feed each other in a continuous cycle.

You can be highly competent in your technical skills the best analyst, engineer, or specialist in your organization and still lack the confidence to lead. Conversely, you can be supremely confident in your ability to influence others yet lack the competence to deliver results. Neither position alone creates effective leadership.

Authentic confidence emerges when competence and self-belief work in harmony. It's the quiet assurance that you can handle what comes not because you know everything, but because you've proven to yourself that you can learn, adapt, and deliver.

Framework: The Confidence Cycle

Building authentic confidence isn't a linear process it's cyclical. Each rotation through this cycle strengthens your foundation and expands your capacity. I call this the Confidence Cycle, and it has five interconnected phases:

1. PREPARATION → 2. ACTION → 3. RESULTS → 4. REFLECTION → 5. GROWTH → (back to PREPARATION)

Phase 1: Preparation

This is where you build competence before the moment demands it. Preparation includes developing technical skills, studying your field, understanding your organization's context, and anticipating challenges.

In my early government career, I didn't wait to be assigned tasks before learning the systems. I studied budget processes, organizational charts, and policy frameworks in advance. When opportunities arose, I was ready not because I was naturally gifted, but because I had prepared.

Key preparation activities:

- Skill development through training, reading, and mentorship
- Understanding your organization's culture, politics, and priorities
- Building relationships before you need them
- Anticipating future challenges and planning responses

PHASE 2: ACTION

This is where Les Brown's wisdom becomes essential: You don't have to be great to get started. Action is the bridge between preparation and confidence. You must throw the rock.

Taking action before you feel completely ready is uncomfortable. Your first presentations may be shaky. Your initial decisions may be questioned. Your early attempts at delegation may require course correction. *This is normal and necessary.*

The leaders who build authentic confidence are those who act despite uncertainty. They raise their hand for the challenging assignment. They speak up in the meeting. They make the call even when the data is incomplete.

Keys to effective action:

- Start with low-stakes opportunities to build momentum
- Focus on progress, not perfection
- Seek feedback early and often
- Embrace the discomfort of growth

PHASE 3: RESULTS

Results provide evidence. Sometimes that evidence confirms your approach worked. Sometimes it reveals what didn't work. Both outcomes are valuable they're data points for your development.

Early in my career as Director of Housing & Community Development, I led an initiative that didn't go as planned. The timeline slipped, stakeholders were frustrated, and I felt like I had failed. But the project ultimately succeeded because we adjusted course based on real-time feedback.

That experience taught me: Results are rarely binary successes or failures. They exist on a spectrum, and your ability to extract lessons from any outcome determines your growth trajectory.

How to assess results productively:

- Separate outcomes from effort (you can do everything right and still face setbacks)
- Look for leading indicators, not just final outcomes
- Celebrate small wins along the way
- Document what worked for future reference

Phase 4: Reflection

Stephen Covey's Habit 7 is "Sharpen the Saw" the practice of continuous renewal and improvement. Reflection is how you sharpen your leadership saw. Without it, you repeat the same patterns without learning from them.

Reflection asks: What did I learn? What would I do differently? What worked better than expected? Where did my assumptions prove wrong? How did others experience my leadership?

I've made reflection a discipline. After significant projects, presentations, or decisions, I take time sometimes just 15 minutes to capture insights while they're fresh. Over the years, these reflections have become invaluable guides.

Effective reflection practices:

- Journal key experiences and lessons learned

- Seek feedback from trusted colleagues and mentors
- Ask better questions: "What surprised me?" not just "Did it work?"
- Review patterns over time, not just individual events

PHASE 5: GROWTH

Growth is where learning converts into capability. You take the insights from reflection and apply them to your next cycle of preparation. Your throwing technique improves. Your distance increases. Your consistency builds.

This is also where confidence compounds. Each successful cycle even ones with setbacks adds evidence to your internal database: "I can handle this. I've done hard things before. I know how to learn and adapt."

The beautiful part of the Confidence Cycle is that it's self-reinforcing. The more you complete the cycle, the more confident you become. And the more confident you become, the bolder actions you're willing to take, which accelerates your growth further.

How to maximize growth:

- Apply lessons immediately to new situations
- Gradually increase the difficulty of challenges you tackle
- Share your learnings with others (teaching solidifies knowledge)
- Celebrate your progress, no matter how incremental

Five Principles of Authentic Confidence

Beyond the Confidence Cycle framework, there are five foundational principles that separate authentic confidence from its counterfeits arrogance, bravado, and false certainty.

Principle 1: Confidence Is Built, Not Born

When people say, "She's a natural leader," what they're really observing is someone who has completed the Confidence Cycle so many times it looks effortless. Behind every "natural" is countless hours of preparation, action, and reflection.

I wasn't naturally confident as a young professional. I was often the quietest person in meetings, uncertain whether my ideas had value. But I committed to building confidence deliberately speaking up once per meeting, then twice, then volunteering for visible projects.

The key insight: If confidence can be built, it can be built by anyone willing to do the work. This democratizes leadership it's not reserved for those born with charisma or privilege.

Principle 2: Confidence Fluctuates And That's Okay

Even seasoned leaders experience confidence dips. A challenging board presentation, a project failure, critical feedback, personal struggles all of these can temporarily shake your self-assurance.

The mistake is believing that confidence should be constant. It's not. What matters is your ability to recognize the dip, understand what's causing it, and take action to rebuild.

During my tenure as Chief of Staff to Governor Parris Glendening, I faced moments of intense scrutiny where my confidence wavered. What helped was returning to fundamentals: reviewing past successes, reconnecting with my preparation, and remembering that one difficult moment doesn't erase years of competence.

Practice: When you feel your confidence slipping, ask yourself, "What evidence do I have of past success?" Ground yourself in facts, not feelings.

PRINCIPLE 3: AUTHENTIC CONFIDENCE INCLUDES HUMILITY

Arrogance says, "I know everything." Authentic confidence says, "I can figure this out, even if I don't know everything right now."

The most confident leaders I've known are also the most curious. They ask questions without shame. They admit when they're wrong. They surround themselves with people smarter than they are. This isn't weakness it's wisdom.

Stephen Covey taught that effective people seek first to understand, then to be understood (Habit 5). This requires the confidence to listen deeply, to value others' perspectives, and to change your mind when presented with better information.

Practice: In your next meeting, commit to asking three genuine questions before offering your opinion. Watch how this builds credibility and confidence simultaneously.

PRINCIPLE 4: YOUR CONFIDENCE AFFECTS OTHERS' PERFORMANCE

During that budget crisis I described in the introduction 37 straight hours, technology failures, impossible deadline I was the only person who genuinely believed we would succeed. But my confidence became contagious.

The team kept working not because they believed in the project's feasibility, but because they believed in me. My certainty gave them permission to keep trying. When they saw I wasn't panicking, they found reserves of energy and creativity they didn't know they had.

This is leadership confidence in action: You hold the belief for the team when they can't hold it for themselves. You become the pole they're aiming at.

Practice: When leading a challenging project, verbalize your confidence explicitly. Say, "I believe we can do this," and explain why. Your team is looking for that signal.

Principle 5: Confidence Requires Context Awareness

Some leaders are confident in technical domains but struggle with political navigation. Others excel at relationship-building but lack confidence in strategic analysis. Authentic confidence recognizes these distinctions.

Throughout my career from county government to state leadership to private sector consulting I've had to recalibrate my confidence for each context. What worked in government didn't automatically translate to airport concessions. Each new environment required a new preparation phase in the Confidence Cycle.

The wisdom is knowing when to lean into your confidence and when to rebuild competence first. Overconfidence in unfamiliar territory is dangerous. Appropriate humility is strength.

Practice: When entering a new role or environment, commit to a 90-day learning phase. Ask questions, observe dynamics, and build competence before making major moves.

Overcoming Impostor Syndrome

If you've ever thought, "I don't belong here," or "They're going to find out I'm not as capable as they think," you've experienced impostor syndrome. Research suggests up to 70% of people experience it at some point.

Impostor syndrome is particularly common among high achievers which means if you're reading this book, you're probably susceptible to it. It often strikes when you're promoted, transitioning to new responsibilities, or operating at the edge of your competence.

Here's what I've learned: Impostor syndrome isn't evidence that you're inadequate. It's evidence that you're growing. It means you're taking on challenges that stretch you, which is exactly where leadership development happens.

Four strategies to manage impostor syndrome:

1. Name it. When you recognize impostor syndrome arising, acknowledge it explicitly: "This is impostor syndrome talking, not reality." This creates distance between you and the feeling.

2. Collect evidence. Keep a "wins file" emails praising your work, successful project outcomes, positive feedback. When impostor syndrome strikes, review this evidence. Your brain needs facts to counter the false narrative.

3. Share it. Talk to trusted colleagues or mentors about your feelings. You'll often discover they've experienced the same doubts. This normalizes the experience and reduces its power.

4. Reframe it. Instead of "I don't belong here," try "I'm learning something new, and discomfort is part of growth." This reframe honors your feelings while maintaining forward momentum.

Remember Les Brown's wisdom: You don't have to be great to get started. Impostor syndrome wants you to wait until you feel great. Don't wait. Start anyway.

AI Applications: Building Confidence with Technology

Artificial intelligence can serve as a powerful accelerator in your confidence-building journey. While AI can't replace the actual work of developing competence and taking action, it can provide tools for self-assessment, practice, feedback, and progress tracking that would have taken me years to develop manually.

Here are specific AI applications for each phase of the Confidence Cycle:

AI Tool 1: Confidence Self-Assessment

Use AI to conduct a comprehensive confidence assessment across different leadership domains. This helps you identify where you're strong and where you need development.

Sample AI Prompt:

"I'm a [your role] leading a team of [number] people in [industry/sector]. Help me assess my leadership confidence across these dimensions: decision-making, public speaking, conflict resolution, strategic planning, delegation, and feedback delivery. For each dimension, ask me 3 questions that will help reveal my current confidence level and underlying competence. Based on my responses, provide specific development recommendations."

This structured assessment gives you a clear starting point and helps you prioritize your development efforts.

AI TOOL 2: PRACTICE SCENARIOS AND SIMULATIONS

One of the most effective ways to build confidence is through practice in low-stakes environments. AI can create realistic scenarios for you to work through before facing them in real life.

Sample AI Prompt:

"I need to deliver difficult feedback to a senior team member who has been underperforming. Simulate this conversation. You play the team member, responding as they realistically might defensively at first, then hopefully more receptively. After our practice conversation, provide specific feedback on my approach, language choices, and opportunities for improvement."

You can practice everything from difficult conversations to board presentations to crisis management decisions. Each practice session builds competence and confidence simultaneously.

AI TOOL 3: REAL-TIME CONFIDENCE COACHING

Before high-stakes moments, presentations, and difficult

conversations, major decisions use AI as a confidence coach to prepare your mindset and strategy.

Sample AI Prompt:

"I'm presenting to our executive team in 2 hours and feeling nervous. The presentation covers [topic] and my biggest concern is [specific worry]. Act as my executive coach. Help me: 1) Reframe my nervousness as positive energy, 2) Identify 3 sources of confidence I can draw on, 3) Anticipate 3 tough questions and help me prepare strong responses, and 4) Give me a 60-second confidence-building visualization to use before I walk in."

This just-in-time coaching can be invaluable when your usual support network isn't available.

AI Tool 4: Progress Tracking and Pattern Recognition

Use AI to track your Confidence Cycle iterations and identify patterns in your development. This makes growth visible and reinforces positive momentum.

Sample AI Prompt:

"I'm going to share my weekly reflections on leadership challenges I faced and how I handled them. After each entry, analyze: 1) Evidence of growth compared to previous weeks, 2) Patterns in situations where I feel most/least confident, 3) Specific competencies that are strengthening, and 4) Recommended focus areas for the coming week. Here's this week's reflection: [your reflection]."

Over time, this creates a rich developmental record that shows your confidence-building journey objectively.

AI TOOL 5: IMPOSTOR SYNDROME COUNTER

When impostor syndrome strikes, use AI to challenge the negative self-talk with evidence-based reality checks.

Sample AI Prompt:

"I'm experiencing impostor syndrome. My negative thoughts are: [list your specific doubts]. Help me counter these with: 1) Objective evidence of my capabilities based on [brief summary of your background], 2) Reframing statements that acknowledge growth while challenging the negative narrative, and 3) Three actions I can take today to rebuild confidence."

Remember: AI is a tool to accelerate your development, not a replacement for the actual work of building confidence through action and reflection. Use these prompts as starting points, then adapt them to your specific context and needs.

Reflection Questions

Take time to think deeply about these questions. Write your responses. The act of writing clarifies thinking and creates accountability.

- Where am I currently in the Confidence Cycle for my most important leadership challenges? Am I stuck in preparation (avoiding action)? Taking action without adequate reflection? Identify your current phase and what needs to happen to move forward.
- When has my confidence been at its highest? What conditions were present? What competencies had I developed? How can I recreate those conditions in my current role?

- In what leadership domains am I most confident? Least confident? What specific actions would build competence (and therefore confidence) in my weak areas?
- How does my confidence (or lack of it) affect my team's performance? Can they sense when I'm uncertain? How might I project appropriate confidence even in ambiguous situations?
- When do I experience impostor syndrome most acutely? What triggers it? What evidence could I collect to counter those feelings?
- If I fully embraced Les Brown's principle "You don't have to be great to get started" what action would I take this week that I've been avoiding?

Action Steps: Building Your Confidence This Week

Knowledge without action is just entertainment. These action steps are designed to move you immediately into the Confidence Cycle. Choose at least two to implement this week.

Action Step 1: Create Your Wins File

Set up a digital folder (or physical file) where you'll collect evidence of your capabilities. Spend 30 minutes right now gathering: positive emails, performance reviews, project successes, testimonials, and awards. Add to this file weekly. Review it whenever confidence wavers.

ACTION STEP 2: IDENTIFY YOUR NEXT GROWTH EDGE

What's one leadership skill just beyond your current comfort zone? Maybe it's public speaking, strategic planning, or difficult conversations. Commit to one low-stakes action this week to practice that skill. Remember: You don't have to be great to get started.

ACTION STEP 3: COMPLETE A CONFIDENCE CYCLE AUDIT

Choose a recent leadership challenge you faced. Map it against the five phases: What preparation did you do? What action did you take? What results occurred? How deeply did you reflect? What growth happened? Identify which phase you're strongest in and which needs more attention.

ACTION STEP 4: PRACTICE WITH AI

Use one of the AI prompts from this chapter to work on a real challenge you're facing. If you have an important meeting coming up, use the Real-Time Confidence Coaching prompt. If you're feeling impostor syndrome, use the Impostor Syndrome Counter. The key is to actually use the tool, not just read about it.

ACTION STEP 5: SHARE YOUR CONFIDENCE JOURNEY

Have a candid conversation with a trusted colleague or mentor about your confidence challenges. Share where you feel strong and where you're working to grow. Ask them to share their own confidence journey. This normalizes the experience and often reveals that even the most confident leaders have doubts.

Chapter Summary: Key Takeaways

- Confidence is built through the Confidence Cycle: Preparation → Action → Results → Reflection → Growth. Each complete cycle strengthens your foundation.
- There is a direct connection between competence and confidence, but you can have one without the other. Authentic leadership requires both working together.
- You don't have to be great to get started, but you have to get started to be great. Action before perfection builds momentum.
- Confidence fluctuates naturally. What matters is your ability to recognize dips and take action to rebuild rather than waiting to "feel confident."
- Authentic confidence includes humility. The most effective leaders combine self-assurance with curiosity and openness to learning.
- Your confidence directly affects your team's performance. When you hold belief for them in difficult moments, you unlock their potential.
- Impostor syndrome is evidence of growth, not inadequacy. Name it, collect counter-evidence, share it with others, and reframe it as part of your development journey.
- AI can accelerate confidence-building through self-assessment, practice scenarios, real-time coaching,

progress tracking, and impostor syndrome countering but it's a tool to support the real work, not replace it.

Building authentic confidence is not a destination it's a practice. Like throwing rocks at telephone poles, you get better with each attempt. The distance increases. The accuracy improves. The confidence compounds.

In the next chapter, we'll build on this foundation by exploring Self-Awareness & Understanding Your Leadership Identity because confidence without self-knowledge is just arrogance in disguise.

Keep throwing.

CHAPTER 2

SELF-AWARENESS & UNDERSTANDING YOUR LEADERSHIP IDENTITY

"Private victories precede public victories.

You can't invert that process any more than you can harvest before you plant."

Stephen R. Covey, The 7 Habits of Highly Effective People

The Mirror and the Window

Early in my career as Director of Housing & Community Development in Prince George's County, I faced a leadership crisis that had nothing to do with budgets, projects, or politics. It had everything to do with a gap I didn't know existed the gap between who I thought I was as a leader and how my team actually experienced me.

I prided myself on being decisive and action-oriented. I saw myself as someone who got things done, who didn't waste time in endless deliberation. In my mind, this was a strength, a source of pride, even.

Then a trusted deputy pulled me aside after a particularly intense meeting. "Major," she said carefully, "Can I be honest with you about something?"

"Always," I replied.

"When you make quick decisions without bringing the team into the process, it feels like you don't value our input. I know that's not your intent, I know you're trying to move us forward efficiently. But the impact is that people feel shut out."

That conversation was a turning point. What I saw in the mirror decisive, efficient leadership was being experienced through the window by my team as exclusionary and dismissive. My *intent* was positive. My *impact* was problematic.

This is the essence of self-awareness: understanding not just who you *think* you are, but who you *actually are* in the experience of others. It's the difference between looking in the mirror and looking through the window.

The Foundation of All Leadership Effectiveness

Stephen Covey teaches that effectiveness is built from the inside out. Before you can lead others effectively, you must understand and lead yourself.

This is Habit 1: Be Proactive taking responsibility for your own life and choices. But you can't be truly proactive without self-awareness.

Self-awareness is the foundation upon which all other leadership capabilities are built. Without it, you're building on sand. Your confidence may be misplaced. Your communication may miss the mark. Your influence may alienate rather than inspire.

T.D. Jakes emphasizes authenticity as central to impactful leadership. But you cannot be authentic if you don't know who you authentically *are*. Authenticity without self-awareness is just consistency in being unaware.

Over four decades of leadership across multiple sectors government, private enterprise, consulting, I've observed a clear pattern: The leaders who rise furthest and sustain their effectiveness longest are not necessarily the smartest or most charismatic. They are the most self-aware.

They know their strengths and leverage them strategically. They know their weaknesses and either develop them or partner with people who complement them.

They understand how they're perceived and adjust their approach accordingly. They recognize their triggers and manage their responses. Most importantly, they remain curious about themselves, always learning, always refining.

Framework: The Leadership Identity Matrix

Your leadership identity exists at the intersection of two dimensions: *who you are* and *how you're seen*. Understanding this intersection and actively working to align these dimensions is the work of developing leadership identity.

The Leadership Identity Matrix has four components:

COMPONENT 1: YOUR INTERNAL IDENTITY (THE MIRROR)

This is who you understand yourself to be your values, beliefs, strengths, motivations, and personal narrative. It includes:

- Core Values: What principles guide your decisions when no one is watching?
- Natural Strengths: What capabilities come easily to you that others struggle with?
- Motivational Drivers: What gives you energy and purpose in your work?
- Personal History: What experiences shaped your leadership approach?
- Leadership Philosophy: What do you believe about how to lead effectively?

For me, my internal identity centers on service, excellence, and empowerment. I believe in making people feel important while coaching them to exceed their own expectations. This isn't something I decided intellectually it emerged from my experiences in public service and was reinforced every time I saw someone flourish under development-focused leadership.

COMPONENT 2: YOUR EXTERNAL PERCEPTION (THE WINDOW)

This is how others actually experience you not what you intend to project, but what they perceive and feel when interacting with you. It includes:

- Behavioral Patterns: What do people consistently observe in how you operate?
- Communication Style: How do others interpret your words, tone, and body language?
- Emotional Impact: What feelings do you tend to evoke in others?
- Reputation: What do people say about you when you're not in the room?
- Perceived Priorities: What do your actions communicate about what you value?

The challenge with external perception is that you can't see it directly you can only learn about it through feedback, observation, and honest reflection. And here's the difficult truth: Your external perception is often more influential than your internal identity in determining your leadership effectiveness.

Component 3: The Alignment Gap

The gap between your internal identity and external perception is where most leadership challenges originate. Consider these common misalignments:

- You see yourself as: *Direct and efficient* | They experience you as: *Abrupt and dismissive*
- You see yourself as: *Collaborative and inclusive* | They experience you as: *Indecisive and slow*
- You see yourself as: *High standards and quality-focused.* They experience you as: *Perfectionist and never satisfied*
- You see yourself as: *Confident and assured* | They experience you as: *Arrogant and closed to input*

- You see yourself as: *Humble and approachable* | They experience you as: *Lacking presence and authority*

Notice: In each case, the internal identity isn't inherently wrong. The problem is the gap the disconnect between intent and impact. Closing this gap requires two actions:

1. Seeking honest feedback about how you're actually perceived

2. Adjusting your behavior to align your impact with your intent

COMPONENT 4: YOUR INTEGRATED IDENTITY (THE IMPACT)

When you successfully align your internal identity with your external perception, you create integrated identity authentic leadership that others can trust and follow.

This is what people mean when they say a leader "walks the talk." There's no disconnect between who they claim to be and how they show up. Their values are visible in their decisions. Their stated priorities match their actual behavior. What they say in public aligns with how they act in private.

This is also what creates the legacy I'm most proud of the fact that former team members say, "Once you work for Major, you always work for Major." That statement reflects integrated identity: My internal commitment to their development was consistently experienced in how I showed up for them, coached them, and advocated for them.

The formula is simple but not easy: Internal Identity + External Perception → Integrated Identity → Leadership Impact

Four Dimensions of Self-Awareness

To develop true self-awareness, you must explore four interconnected dimensions. Each reveals different truths about who you are as a leader.

Dimension 1: Know Your Strengths (And How to Leverage Them)

Early in my career, I spent significant energy trying to be good at everything. I worked on my weaknesses relentlessly while taking my strengths for granted. This was exhausting and inefficient.

The breakthrough came when I shifted focus: Instead of trying to eliminate weaknesses, I doubled down on strengths while managing around weaknesses through team composition and partnerships.

My natural strengths include:

- Strategic anticipation seeing needs before they become crises
- Relationship building connecting with people across hierarchies and sectors
- Operational execution getting complex projects across the finish line
- People development coaching individuals to exceed their own expectations

Once I recognized these patterns, I could position myself strategically. I took roles where these strengths mattered most. I surrounded myself with people who brought complementary capabilities detailed analysts, creative visionaries, and technical specialists who balanced my profile.

Questions to identify your strengths:

- What comes easily to you that others struggle with?
- What tasks give you energy rather than draining you?
- What do people consistently ask for your help with?
- When have you been most successful, and what strengths were you using?

DIMENSION 2: KNOW YOUR BLIND SPOTS (AND HOW THEY TRIP YOU UP)

Blind spots are the gaps in your self-awareness behaviors, patterns, and impacts that others see clearly but you don't recognize. They're called blind spots precisely because you can't see them on your own.

Remember my story about being perceived as exclusionary when I thought I was being efficient? That was a blind spot. I genuinely didn't realize how my quick decision-making affected team morale. It took brave feedback from a trusted deputy to reveal it.

Common leadership blind spots include:

- Speaking more than listening in meetings
- Unconsciously favoring certain team members
- Micromanaging when stressed
- Dismissing ideas that aren't immediately clear
- Creating urgency that feels like chaos to others
- Avoiding conflict until problems escalate

The only way to discover blind spots is through external feedback 360-degree reviews, trusted advisors, team retrospectives, or professional coaching. This requires vulnerability and courage. It's uncomfortable to hear that your well-intentioned behavior is creating negative impacts.

But here's the gift: Once a blind spot is revealed, it's no longer blind. You can manage it, mitigate it, or change it. The awareness itself is transformative.

How to uncover your blind spots:

- Actively seeking feedback from multiple sources
- Pay attention to repeated patterns in feedback, even if subtle
- Notice where you get defensive that's often revealing
- Ask directly: "What do I do that frustrates you?"

Dimension 3: Know Your Triggers (And How to Manage Them)

Triggers are situations, behaviors, or dynamics that provoke disproportionate emotional responses in you. When triggered, you're no longer responding to the present moment you're reacting from past experiences, unhealed wounds, or deep-seated fears.

I know my triggers well now, but only because I've done the hard work of identifying them:

- Being blindsided When important information is withheld from me, I react with frustration. This stems from early career experiences where lack of information hurt my ability to lead effectively.

- Mediocrity accepted as good enough When people settle for less than their capability, I struggle with patience. My drive for excellence can sometimes feel like pressure to others.
- Lack of follow-through When commitments aren't honored, I take it personally. This reflects my own deep commitment to reliability and integrity.

Knowing these triggers doesn't eliminate them, but it gives me space to respond rather than react. When I feel that surge of frustration about being blindsided, I can recognize: "This is my trigger. Pause. Breathe. Respond from my values, not my wounds."

Covey teaches this as the space between stimulus and response where our freedom and growth lie. Self-aware leaders expand that space through conscious practice.

Questions to identify your triggers:

- When do I overreact compared to the situation's actual stakes?
- What behaviors in others consistently frustrate me?
- What situations make me want to shut down or lash out?
- What patterns from my past still show up in my present reactions?

DIMENSION 4: KNOW YOUR VALUES (AND WHETHER YOU LIVE THEM)

Many leaders can articulate their values intellectually integrity, excellence, service, and innovation. But the real question isn't what values you *claim*, it's what values you *demonstrate* through your actual decisions and behaviors.

T.D. Jakes teaches that authentic leadership requires alignment between your stated values and your lived experience. When there's a gap when you say one thing but do another people notice. And they lose trust.

My core values have remained consistent throughout my career:

- Service Leadership is fundamentally about serving others, not being served
- Excellence Mediocrity is a choice; we can always deliver more value
- Development People have untapped potential that coaching can unlock
- Integrity Your word is your bond; reliability builds trust
- Anticipation Leaders solve problems before they become crises

But values mean nothing if they're not visible in your behavior. That budget crisis I described earlier. That was my values in action: Service (staying with the team through exhaustion), Excellence (refusing to accept anything less than on-time delivery), Development (coaching team members through doubt), and Integrity (honoring our commitment to stakeholders).

The team didn't need to ask what I valued, they saw it demonstrated in real-time crisis conditions. That's when values become credible.

Test for values alignment:

- List of your top 5 stated values
- Review your calendar and budget from last month, what do they reveal about your actual priorities?
- Ask your team: "Based on my behavior, what would you say I value most?"
- Where's the gap? That's where development work needs to happen.

Building the Habit of Self-Awareness

Self-awareness isn't a one-time achievement, it's continuous practice. Like physical fitness, it requires regular exercise to maintain and strengthen. Here are four practices that have sustained my own self-awareness journey:

Practice 1: Daily Reflection

Spend 10-15 minutes at the end of each day reviewing key interactions and decisions. Ask: What went well? What could I have handled differently? What did I learn about myself today? This isn't about perfectionism it's about continuous learning.

Practice 2: Seek Regular Feedback

Build feedback into your leadership rhythm. After significant projects, meetings, or presentations, ask specific questions: "What did you observe about my approach? What worked well? What could I improve?" Make it safe for people to be honest.

Practice 3: Study Your Patterns

Keep a leadership journal. Over time, patterns emerge situations where you consistently excel, triggers that repeatedly challenge you, blind spots that need ongoing attention. Pattern recognition accelerates growth.

Practice 4: Invest in External Perspective

Work with a coach, mentor, or trusted advisor who can provide objective insights about your development. The investment pays dividends external perspective reveals what internal reflection cannot.

AI Applications: Accelerating Self-Awareness with Technology

AI can serve as a powerful mirror for self-awareness development. While it can't replace human feedback and genuine self-reflection, it can provide structured analysis, pattern recognition, and developmental insights that would take years to accumulate manually.

Here are five AI applications specifically designed for building self-awareness:

AI Tool 1: Leadership Identity Assessment

Use AI to conduct a comprehensive assessment of your leadership identity across the four dimensions we've explored.

Sample AI Prompt:

"I'm a [role] leading [context]. Help me develop deeper self-awareness by walking me through the four dimensions: 1) My strengths and how to leverage them, 2) My potential blind spots based on my role and tendencies, 3) My likely triggers given my background in [brief background], and 4) My stated vs. lived values. For each dimension, ask me 3-4 probing questions, then provide analysis and development recommendations based on my responses."

This structured conversation creates a baseline self-awareness assessment you can revisit quarterly to track growth.

AI TOOL 2: 360-DEGREE FEEDBACK SIMULATOR

While AI can't replace real 360-degree feedback, it can help you prepare for it by simulating perspectives from different stakeholders.

Sample AI Prompt:

"I'm preparing for a 360-degree feedback process. Based on my role as [role] and my leadership approach [brief description], simulate feedback I might receive from: 1) My direct reports, 2) My peers, 3) My supervisor, and 4) External stakeholders. For each perspective, provide 2-3 areas of strength they'd likely note and 2-3 areas for development. Then help me prepare productive responses to potential challenging feedback."

This preparation helps you approach real feedback with openness rather than defensiveness.

AI TOOL 3: BLIND SPOT IDENTIFICATION THROUGH BEHAVIORAL ANALYSIS

Use AI to analyze patterns in your behavior descriptions and identify potential blind spots.

Sample AI Prompt:

"I'm going to describe how I typically handle [specific leadership situation, e.g., team meetings, conflict, delegation]. As I describe my approach, identify potential blind spots gaps between my intent and likely impact, behaviors I might not recognize, or patterns that could create unintended consequences. Here's my description: [your detailed description]. What blind spots do you see, and what specific feedback questions should I ask my team to validate these?"

The key is being honest in your description AI can only work with what you share.

AI Tool 4: Values Alignment Audit

Use AI to assess the gap between your stated values and your actual behaviors.

Sample AI Prompt:

"My stated leadership values are: [list your values]. Here's how I spent my time last week: [brief calendar review]. Here are three recent significant decisions I made: [describe decisions]. Analyze the alignment between my stated values and my actual behaviors. Where is alignment strong? Where are gaps? What specific behavior changes would better demonstrate my stated values?"

This audit reveals whether you're walking your talk and where adjustments are needed.

AI Tool 5: Pattern Recognition in Leadership Journal

Use AI to analyze your leadership reflections over time and identify patterns you might miss.

Sample AI Prompt:

"I've been keeping a leadership journal. I'm going to share entries from the past month. Analyze them for patterns: 1) Recurring themes in my challenges, 2) Situations where I consistently thrive vs. struggle, 3) Emotional triggers that appear repeatedly, 4) Evidence of growth or areas where I'm stuck. Here are my entries: [paste entries]. What patterns do you see that I should pay attention to?"

This longitudinal analysis reveals trends that are hard to see in the moment-to-moment experience of leadership.

Reflection Questions

These questions are designed to deepen your self-awareness. Take time with them superficial answers produce superficial growth.

- What's the biggest gap between who I think I am as a leader and how my team likely experiences me? What evidence do I have for this gap?
- Which of my strengths do I leverage well? Which strengths am I underutilizing? How could I amplify their impact?
- What blind spots might I have that I haven't uncovered yet? Who in my network would tell me the truth if I asked the right questions?
- What consistently triggers me in leadership situations? What past experiences or fears drive these reactions? How can I create space between trigger and response?
- Are my stated values actually visible in my calendar, budget, and daily decisions? Where is the alignment strong? Where is it weak?
- If I committed to one year of intensive self-awareness development, what would change in my leadership?

What impact would that have on my team and organization?

Action Steps: Deepening Your Self-Awareness This Week

Self-awareness develops through deliberate practice, not passive reading. Choose at least two of these action steps to implement immediately.

Action Step 1: Conduct Your Leadership Identity Audit

Use the Leadership Identity Matrix framework. Write down: 1) Who you believe you are as a leader (internal identity), 2) How you think others perceive you (external perception), and 3) Where you suspect gaps exist. Then validate your assumptions by asking 2-3 trusted colleagues for honest feedback.

Action Step 2: Identify Your Top 3 Blind Spots

Schedule three 30-minute conversations with people who see you lead regularly a peer, a direct report, and your supervisor if possible. Ask them specifically: "What do I do that I might not realize affects the team negatively?" Listen without defending or explaining. Just collect the data.

Action Step 3: Map Your Triggers and Create Response Strategies

Make a list of situations that consistently provoke strong emotional reactions in you. For each trigger, identify: 1) The underlying fear or past experience driving it, 2) Your typical reactive behavior, 3) A more effective response you'd like to cultivate. Practice the new response through mental rehearsal.

Action Step 4: Values Alignment Check

Review your calendar and budget from last month. What do they reveal about your actual priorities? Compare this to your stated values. Where's the alignment? Where's the gap? Make one specific change this week to better align your behavior with your values.

Action Step 5: Start a Self-Awareness Journal

Commit to 10 minutes of daily reflection for the next 30 days. Each day, answer: What did I learn about myself today? Where did my behavior align with my values? Where was there a gap? What pattern am I noticing? The compound effect of this practice is transformative.

Chapter Summary: Key Takeaways

- Self-awareness is the foundation of all leadership effectiveness. Without it, you're building on sand your other capabilities can't reach their full potential.
- The Leadership Identity Matrix shows that your impact is determined by the intersection of your internal identity (who you are) and external perception (how you're seen). Closing the gap between these creates authentic, integrated leadership.
- Self-awareness has four critical dimensions: knowing your strengths, identifying your blind spots, understanding your triggers, and ensuring your values are lived, not just stated.
- Blind spots can only be revealed through external feedback. The courage to seek and receive honest

feedback is what separates developing leaders from stagnant ones.

- Triggers are situations that provoke disproportionate emotional responses. Identifying and managing them expands the space between stimulus and response where leadership effectiveness lives.
- Your stated values mean nothing if they're not visible in your actual behavior. Authentic leadership requires alignment between what you say and what you do, especially under pressure.
- Self-awareness is a continuous practice, not a destination. Daily reflection, regular feedback, pattern study, and external perspective are the habits that sustain growth.
- AI can accelerate self-awareness through identity assessments, blind spot analysis, values audits, and pattern recognition but it supplements, not replaces, human feedback and genuine reflection.

Stephen Covey was right: Private victories precede public victories. The work of understanding yourself truly seeing yourself with clarity and honesty is private work. But it's the foundation for every public success you'll achieve as a leader.

In the next chapter, we'll explore how to take your self-awareness and authentic confidence into the realm of Communication That Drives High Performance because knowing yourself is only valuable if you can translate that knowledge into effective interaction with others.

The journey inward creates the capacity for the journey outward.

CHAPTER 3

COMMUNICATION THAT DRIVES HIGH PERFORMANCE

Seek first to understand, then to be understood."

Stephen R. Covey, Habit 5

The Message You Send vs. The Message They Receive

During my time as Director of Budget & Management in Prince George's County, I called what I thought was a straightforward meeting to discuss budget allocation adjustments. Several departments would need to reduce their requests by 5-8% to balance the overall budget. I had the numbers, the rationale, and the solution clearly mapped out.

I opened the meeting by presenting the financial reality: revenue projections were down, fixed costs were up, and we needed to make strategic cuts.

I walked through my recommended reductions department by department. The numbers were fair, the analysis was sound, and the plan was workable.

But as I presented, I noticed the energy in the room shift. Department heads who are usually engaged actively sat back with crossed arms. Facial expressions ranged from resignation to resentment. When I asked questions, the silence was heavy.

After the meeting, one director pulled me aside. "Major," he said, "I respect your analysis. But you just told us what's going to happen rather than asking for our input. These cuts will affect real programs and real people. We needed to be part of the solution, not just informed of your decision."

He was absolutely right.

I had communicated *information* efficiently. But I had failed to communicate *respect, partnership, and shared ownership* which is what the situation actually required.

The message I *intended to send* was: "Here's a fair, well-analyzed solution to our challenge." The message they *actually received* was: "Your input doesn't matter. This decision has already been made."

This experience taught me a fundamental truth about leadership communication: The effectiveness of your communication is measured not by what you say, but by what others hear, understand, and feel moved to act upon.

Communication: The Leader's Primary Tool

Leadership is fundamentally an act of communication. Everything you accomplish as a leader vision-setting, strategy execution, team development, change management, crisis response happens through communication.

You can have brilliant strategy, but if you can't communicate it compellingly, it remains locked in your head. You can identify the right priorities, but if your team doesn't understand them clearly, they'll work on the wrong things. You can have deep care for your people, but if you don't express it effectively, they'll never feel it.

John Maxwell teaches that leadership influences nothing more, nothing less. And how do you influence? Through communication. Your words, tone, body language, listening, questions, feedback, and presence are the tools through which influence flows.

Yet many leaders underinvest in communication skills. They assume that being articulate or having technical expertise is sufficient. It's not. Effective leadership communication requires:

- Intentionality about what you want to accomplish
- Awareness of your audience's needs and perspectives
- Clarity in message structure and delivery
- Skill in reading and adapting to real-time feedback
- Commitment to follow-through and accountability

In this chapter, I'll share a framework that has transformed how I communicate as a leader a framework that turns communication from an afterthought into a strategic capability that drives high performance.

Framework: The CLEAR Communication Model

High-performance communication follows a predictable pattern. Whether you're delivering feedback, presenting strategy, facilitating meetings, or navigating conflict, the same five elements determine effectiveness. I call this the CLEAR Communication Model:

C - Context | L - Listen | E - Engage | A - Align | R - Results

C - Context: Frame the Conversation

Before diving into content, establish context. Context answers the questions your audience is already asking (consciously or unconsciously):

- Why are we having this conversation?
- What's at stake?
- How does this connect to our larger goals?
- What's my role in this discussion?
- What outcome are we working toward?

Without context, people fill in the blanks with assumptions and assumptions are rarely accurate. When I failed to provide context in that budget meeting, directors assumed I had made unilateral decisions. The assumption created resistance before I even presented the details.

How I should have opened that meeting:

"Thank you all for being here. We're facing a budget

challenge that requires creative thinking from all of us. Revenue projections are down 8%, and we need to balance the budget without compromising our core mission. I've done preliminary analysis, but I need your expertise to refine these recommendations and ensure we're making the right cuts in the right places. The goal of this meeting is to collaborate on a solution we can all support. Let me share what I'm seeing, then I want to hear your perspectives."

Same content. Completely different context. This framing invites collaboration rather than triggering resistance.

Practice: Before your next important conversation, write a 2-3 sentence context statement. Include the purpose, stakes, and desired outcome. Start with this framing before presenting content.

L - LISTEN: SEEK TO UNDERSTAND FIRST

This is Covey's Habit 5 in action: Seek first to understand, then to be understood. Most leaders reverse this order they seek first to be understood, then wonder why people resist their perfectly logical arguments.

Effective listening isn't passive, it's active and intentional. It requires temporarily setting aside your agenda to fully understand another person's perspective, concerns, and motivations.

I've learned to distinguish between three levels of listening:

Level 1: Waiting to Talk - You're not really listening. You're rehearsing your response while they speak. This is the most common form of "listening" and the least effective.

Level 2: Listening for Content - You're hearing the words and tracking the information. This is necessary but insufficient. Content without context and emotion is incomplete.

Level 3: Listening for Meaning - You're hearing the content AND paying attention to emotions, concerns, and underlying needs. You're asking: What's really being said here? What matters most to this person? What are they worried about? This is leadership-level listening.

In that budget meeting, if I had listened at Level 3, I would have heard the unspoken concern: "We want to be part of solving this problem, not just recipients of your solution." Addressing that concern would have changed the entire dynamic.

Techniques for Level 3 listening:

- Paraphrase and reflect: "What I'm hearing is... Is that accurate?"
- Name emotions: "It sounds like you're frustrated about... Tell me more."
- Ask clarifying questions: "Help me understand what concerns you most about this."
- Resist the urge to solve it immediately: "Let me make sure I fully understand before we talk about solutions."
- Practice silence: After someone speaks, pause for 2-3 seconds before responding. This signals you're processing, not just waiting for your turn.

E - Engage: Create Dialogue, Not Monologue

Engagement transforms communication from transmission (one-way) to collaboration (two-way). When you engage people authentically, you tap into their insights, creativity, and commitment.

The most powerful tool for engagement? Questions. Great leaders don't just make statements, they ask questions that invite thinking, participation, and ownership.

Consider these two approaches to the same situation:

Approach 1 (Low Engagement): "We need to improve our customer response time. I've decided we'll implement a new ticketing system and hire two additional support staff. Training starts next month."

Approach 2 (High Engagement): "Our customer response time is a concern we're averaging 48 hours when our goal is 24. What's causing this gap? [Listen] Given those constraints, what solutions might address both the volume issue and the complexity issue? [Listen] If we implemented those changes, what would success look like? What support would you need?"

The second approach takes longer initially. But it creates buy-in, surfaces insights you might have missed, and builds capability in your team to think strategically. The time you invest in engagement pays dividends in execution.

Questions that drive engagement:

- "What's your perspective on this?"
- "What am I missing?"
- "If you were making this decision, what would you consider?"
- "What concerns do you have about this approach?"
- "How can we make this even better?"

Note: Engagement requires genuine curiosity. If you're asking questions but have already decided the answer, people will sense it. The questions must be authentic invitations for input.

A - Align: Create Shared Understanding

Alignment is where communication often breaks down. You think you've been clear. Your team thinks they understand. Then execution reveals you were talking about different things. Alignment requires explicit confirmation not assumption that everyone shares the same understanding of:

- What success looks like
- Who's responsible for what
- What the timeline is
- What resources are available
- What the priorities are

I learned to test for alignment by asking people to summarize back to me what they heard. Early in my career, this felt awkward like I was treating people like children. But I discovered it wasn't about doubting their intelligence; it was about ensuring we were starting from the same place.

Here's what testing for alignment sounds like:

"Before we wrap up, let me make sure we're aligned. Can you summarize what you're taking on, your deadline, and what success looks like? I want to confirm I've communicated clearly."

Notice the framing: "I want to confirm I've communicated clearly" not "I want to make sure you understood." The former puts responsibility on you (where it belongs), while the latter sounds condescending.

Often, when people summarize back, you'll discover gaps you didn't realize existed. They emphasize different aspects than you intended. They make assumptions you didn't anticipate. This is gold, it's the opportunity to correct misalignment before it becomes a problem.

Techniques for ensuring alignment:

- Summarize key points yourself before asking others to confirm
- Use written follow-up to document agreements (email, shared doc, project plan)
- Check in early in execution don't wait until the deadline to discover misalignment
- Create visual representations when possible (diagrams, timelines, org charts)

R - RESULTS: FOLLOW THROUGH AND CLOSE THE LOOP

Communication doesn't end when the conversation ends. It ends when results are achieved and learning is captured. This final element follow-through is where average leaders fall short and exceptional leaders excel.

Results focused communication include:

1. Track commitments made during conversations and hold people (including yourself) accountable to them.

2. Provide progress updates so people know their work matters and the larger initiative is moving forward.

3. Celebrate wins publicly to reinforce desired behaviors and outcomes.

4. Address gaps quickly when commitments aren't met not with blame, but with curiosity about what's getting in the way.

5. Close the loop by sharing what happened as a result of the conversation and what was learned.

Remember that budget meeting I opened poorly? After the director gave me honest feedback, I didn't just apologize I took action. I scheduled a follow-up session where department heads collaborated on the recommendations. We refined the approach together, and I explicitly credited their input in the final presentation to county leadership.

Then I closed the loop: I sent a note thanking them for their partnership and acknowledging that my initial approach had been wrong. This demonstrated that I valued their feedback and was willing to adjust which strengthened trust for future difficult conversations.

Results-focused communication builds credibility over time. Your team learns that when you say something will happen, it does. When you ask for input, you actually use it. When you commit to follow-through, you deliver. This credibility is leadership currency.

Practice: After every significant conversation, create a simple tracking system: What was committed? By whom? By when? Then follow up proactively rather than waiting for people to come to you.

Adapting Your Communication Style

The CLEAR model provides structure, but effective communication also requires flexibility. Different situations, audiences, and individuals require different approaches.

Throughout my career across government, private sector, and consulting, I've learned to read the room and adapt my style accordingly:

Crisis Communication: Be direct, decisive, and calm. People need clarity and confidence, not extensive consultation. Save the detailed explanations for after the crisis passes.

Strategic Communication: Paint the big picture first, then drill into details. Connect strategy to individual roles. Use stories and examples to make abstract concepts concrete.

Developmental Communication: Ask questions more than you give answers. Create space for people to think through problems. Your goal is capability-building, not problem-solving.

Difficult Communication: Lead with respect and specific observations. Separate behavior from character. End with clear expectations and support for improvement.

Celebratory Communication: Be generous and specific. Public praise should far outweigh public criticism. Make people feel genuinely appreciated, not just checked off a list. The key is intentionality. Before important communications, ask yourself:

- What's the situation demanding?
- What does my audience need?
- What style will be most effective here?
- How can I adapt while staying authentic?

Mastering Difficult Conversations

One of the clearest differentiators between average and exceptional leaders is their ability to have difficult conversations well. Most leaders avoid these conversations until they become crises. Exceptional leaders lean into them early.

What makes a conversation "difficult"? Usually it's one or more of these factors:

- The content is sensitive (performance issues, behavior concerns)
- The stakes are high (decisions with major consequences)
- Emotions are involved (conflict, disappointment, fear)
- Power dynamics are at play (managing up, peer conflict)

I've developed a four-step approach for difficult conversations that honors both truth and relationship:

Step 1: Prepare Your Mindset

Before the conversation, get clear on your intent. Are you trying to punish or develop? Prove you're right or find the truth? Win or solve? Your mindset shapes everything that follows. The most effective mindset: "I care about this person AND the organization's success. How can I address this issue while preserving dignity and relationship?"

Step 2: Open with Respect and Specificity

Begin by acknowledging the person's value and your positive intent. Then state the specific concern without judgment. Compare these openings:

Poor: "We need to talk about your attitude problem."

Better: "I value your contributions to this team, and I want to discuss something I've observed that concerns me. In the last three team meetings, when others have shared ideas, you've responded with criticism before asking questions. This is creating tension. Can we talk about what's happening?"

STEP 3: LISTEN TO THEIR PERSPECTIVE

After stating your concern, genuinely seek to understand their experience. Often, difficult behaviors have underlying causes you don't know about personal stress, unclear expectations, feeling undervalued, or conflicting priorities. This doesn't excuse the behavior, but it provides context for addressing it effectively.

STEP 4: ALIGN ON PATH FORWARD

End with clear expectations and support. What specifically needs to change? What will you do to help? How will you measure progress? When will you check in again? Document this agreement and follow through.

The goal of difficult conversations isn't to be liked, it's to be respected. People may not enjoy the conversation, but they should leave clear on expectations and believing you care about their success.

AI Applications: Enhancing Communication with Technology

AI can significantly enhance your communication effectiveness by helping you prepare, practice, analyze, and improve. While AI can't replace authentic human connection, it can serve as a powerful tool for developing communication skills and crafting more effective messages.

Here are five AI applications for communication excellence:

AI Tool 1: Message Clarity Analyzer

Before important communications, use AI to analyze your draft for clarity, tone, and potential misinterpretations.

Sample AI Prompt:

"I'm about to send this message to my team about [topic]. Analyze it for:

1) Clarity are their ambiguous terms or unclear expectations.

2) How will this likely be received emotionally?

3) Completeness what questions might people have that I haven't answered?

4) Potential misinterpretations how might this be misunderstood?

This analysis often reveals gaps you miss because you know what you mean but your audience doesn't have your context.

AI Tool 2: Difficult Conversation Simulator

Practice difficult conversations in a safe environment before having them in real life.

Sample AI Prompt:

"I need to have a difficult conversation with [role/person type] about [specific issue]. The person tends to be [describe their typical communication style/reactions. Simulate this conversation you play them, I'll respond. React realistically including potential defensiveness, emotion, or misunderstanding. After our practice conversation, provide feedback on 1) What I did well, 2) Where I could improve, 3) Specific phrases or approaches that would be more effective. Let's begin."

This practice builds confidence and helps you anticipate reactions, so you're not caught off guard.

AI TOOL 3: COMMUNICATION STYLE ADAPTER

Adapt your communication style for different audiences while maintaining your authentic voice.

Sample AI Prompt:

"I need to communicate [same message/decision] to three different audiences: 1) My team (direct reports), 2) Senior leadership (executives), and 3) External stakeholders (clients/partners). Here's the core message: [your message]. Help me adapt this for each audience, adjusting tone, level of detail, emphasis points, and length while maintaining consistency in the key information. Show me three versions."

This helps you tailor communication without losing essential meaning across different contexts.

AI TOOL 4: MEETING FACILITATION PLANNER

Design meetings that drive engagement and alignment using the CLEAR model.

Sample AI Prompt:

"I'm facilitating a meeting about [topic] with [number/type of participants]. The goal is [specific outcome]. Using the CLEAR Communication Model (Context, Listen, Engage, Align, Results), help me design this meeting: 1) Opening context statement, 2) Questions to prompt listening and engagement, 3) Techniques to ensure alignment, 4) How to close with clear next steps.

Include timing for each element. Total meeting time: [X minutes]."

This structured approach transforms meetings from timewasters into productivity engines.

AI Tool 5: Communication Pattern Analyzer

Analyze your communication patterns over time to identify strengths and blind spots.

Sample AI Prompt:

"I'm going to share examples of my recent communications (emails, messages, meeting notes). Analyze them for patterns:

1) Do I tend toward too much or too little detail?

2) Is my tone consistently appropriate or does it vary unpredictably?

3) Do I follow through on commitments made?

4) Where do I excel in communication?

5) What consistent gaps or weaknesses appear? Here are my examples:

This meta-analysis reveals patterns you can't see when you're in the moment, accelerating your development.

Reflection Questions

Use these questions to assess and improve your communication effectiveness.

- Think about a recent important communication that didn't go as planned. Which element of the CLEAR model was weakest? What specifically could you have done differently?

- How often do I truly listen at Level 3 (for meaning) versus Level 1 (waiting to talk) or Level 2 (content only)? What gets in the way of deeper listening?
- When I communicate, do I prioritize being understood or understanding others first? How might reversing that order change my effectiveness?
- What difficult conversation have I been avoiding? What's the cost of continued avoidance versus the discomfort of addressing it now?
- Do I consistently follow through on communication commitments (responding when I say I will, providing updates, closing loops)? Where do I fall short?
- If I asked my team to rate my communication effectiveness on a scale of 1-10, what would they say? What specific evidence would support their rating?

Action Steps: Improving Your Communication This Week

Communication skills improve through deliberate practice. Choose at least two action steps to implement immediately.

ACTION STEP 1: PRACTICE THE CLEAR MODEL

Before your next important meeting or conversation, explicitly plan how you'll address each element: Context (how will you frame it?), Listen (what questions will you ask?), Engage (how will you invite participation?), Align (how will you confirm understanding?), Results (how will you track follow-through?). Use a simple template to prepare.

Action Step 2: Conduct a Communication Audit

Review your communications from the past week (emails, messages, meetings). Rate yourself on each CLEAR element. Where are you strong? Where do you consistently underperform? Choose one element to focus on improving this month.

Action Step 3: Practice Level 3 Listening

In your next three conversations, commit to listening for meaning, not just content. After each conversation, reflect: What emotions did I notice? What underlying concerns did they have? What did they need that wasn't explicitly stated? How did listening more deeply change the interaction?

Action Step 4: Have That Difficult Conversation

Identify one difficult conversation you've been avoiding. Use the four-step approach: 1) Prepare your mindset (care + clarity), 2) Open with respect and specificity, 3) Listen to their perspective, 4) Align on path forward. Schedule it within 48 hours before you talk yourself out of it.

Action Step 5: Test for Alignment

After delegating work or setting expectations, ask the person to summarize back what they heard. Use the non-condescending framing: "Let me make sure I've communicated clearly can you summarize what you're taking on?" Notice what gets emphasized differently than you intended and clarify immediately.

Chapter Summary: Key Takeaways

- Communication is the leader's primary tool. Everything you accomplish happens through communication vision, strategy, development, change, and crisis response.
- Effectiveness is measured not by what you say, but by what others hear, understand, and feel moved to act upon. Intent doesn't equal impact.
- The CLEAR Communication Model provides structure: Context (frame it), Listen (understand first), Engage (create dialogue), Align (confirm understanding), Results (follow through).
- Level 3 listening for meaning, not just content is what separates good communicators from great ones. It requires genuine curiosity about what matters to others.
- Engagement transforms communication from transmission to collaboration. Questions are more powerful than statements for creating buy-in and surfacing insights.
- Alignment requires explicit confirmation, not assumption. Test understanding by having people summarize back what they heard.
- Difficult conversations separate average from exceptional leaders. The four-step approach: prepare mindset, open with respect, listen to perspective, align on path forward.
- Follow-through closes the loop. Track commitments, provide updates, celebrate wins, address gaps quickly,

and share what was learned. This builds credibility over time.

- AI can enhance communication through message analysis, conversation practice, style adaptation, meeting design, and pattern recognition but it supplements authentic connection, not replaces it.

Stephen Covey's Habit 5 Seek first to understand, then to be understood isn't just good advice. It's the foundation of high-performance communication. When you genuinely understand what matters to others before pushing your own agenda, you create the conditions for alignment, engagement, and results.

In the next chapter, we'll explore Adaptability in Changing Environments because even the best communication requires flexibility when circumstances shift rapidly. The ability to read context and adjust your approach is what allows confident, self-aware leaders to thrive in uncertainty.

Communication is not what you say. It's what they hear. Master that difference.

CHAPTER 4

ADAPTABILITY IN CHANGING ENVIRONMENTS

"It is not the strongest of the species that survives,

nor the most intelligent, but the one most responsive to change."

Charles Darwin

When the Ground Shifts Beneath You

In 2001, I was serving as Chief of Technology and Chair of Maryland's Information Technology Board, leading the state's digital transformation initiatives. We had ambitious plans, solid budgets, and strong momentum. Then the financial crisis hit.

Within weeks, everything changed. Budget projections collapsed. Hiring freezes were implemented. Projects we'd spent months planning were suddenly unfunded. The technology landscape was shifting rapidly, but our resources to respond were evaporating.

I watched some leaders freeze paralyzed by the sudden shift, waiting for conditions to return to "normal." Others panicked, making reactive decisions that created more problems than they solved. A few tried to power through with the original plan, as if sheer willpower could overcome the new reality.

None of these responses worked.

What did work was rapid adaptation. We stepped back and asked: Given this new reality, what's most important? What can we accomplish with constrained resources? How can we deliver more value with less investment?

We pivoted from large infrastructure projects to high-impact, low-cost initiatives. We accelerated cloud adoption to reduce capital expenditure. We partnered with other state agencies to share resources. We automated routine processes to free up staff for strategic work. We shifted from "How do we do everything we planned?" to "How do we maximize impact with what we have?"

The crisis forced innovation. Some of our most effective solutions emerged not despite the constraints, but *because of* them. We emerged from that period stronger, leaner, and more adaptable than before.

This experience taught me a crucial leadership truth: Adaptability isn't just a nice-to-have capability, it's a survival requirement. The leaders who thrive over decades aren't those with perfect plans. They're those who can read about changing conditions, let go of what's no longer working, and pivot to new approaches without losing their core purpose.

Leadership as a Fluid Process

As I mentioned in the introduction, leadership isn't a one-time event, it's a fluid process with constantly changing conditions. Sometimes things flow smoothly. Sometimes you throw a little too hard and miss the target. Confidence fluctuates based on performance, assignment size, mistakes made, and the support you receive.

The word "fluid" is carefully chosen. Fluids adapt to their container water takes the shape of whatever vessel holds it. Rigid objects break when conditions change; fluid substances flow and adjust.

Throughout my career across multiple sectors, county government, state leadership, private enterprise, airport concessions, consulting, I've observed that organizational environments are increasingly fluid. Technology disrupts business models overnight. Economic conditions shift rapidly. Regulatory landscapes evolve. Stakeholder expectations change. Competitive threats emerge from unexpected directions.

In this reality, your ability to adapt determines your survival and success. The specific skills that got you to your current role won't necessarily carry you forward. The strategies that worked last year may be irrelevant this year. The leadership style that was effective in one environment may fall flat in another.

T.D. Jakes teaches that resilience, the ability to bounce back from setbacks and adapt to change is essential for impactful leadership. But resilience isn't just about recovery; it's about transformation. It's not returning to your previous state; it's evolving into something stronger and more capable.

Framework: The Adaptability Compass

Adaptability isn't random flexibility, it's disciplined responsiveness. You're not changing direction arbitrarily; you're navigating intentionally toward your destination despite shifting conditions. I call this framework the Adaptability Compass because it helps you find true north even when the landscape around you is in flux.

The Adaptability Compass has four directional points:

CONTEXT → ASSESSMENT → ADJUSTMENT → ACTION

North: Context - Read the Environment

Before you can adapt effectively, you must understand what's actually happening. This requires careful reading of your environment across multiple dimensions:

External Context: Market conditions, competitive landscape, regulatory environment, technological trends, economic factors, social dynamics

Internal Context: Organizational culture, team capability, resource availability, political dynamics, operational capacity, strategic priorities

Temporal Context: Where are we in the organizational lifecycle? What season are we in? Is this a sprint or a marathon? Is this change temporary or permanent?

During the 2008 crisis, reading context meant recognizing that this wasn't a temporary dip it was a fundamental shift that would reshape government technology budgets for years. Leaders who misread this context and planned for a quick return to previous funding levels wasted time and energy on strategies that were no longer viable.

Questions for reading context:

- What's actually changing vs. what feels like it's changing?
- Is this change temporary or permanent?
- What signals am I missing because they don't fit my expectations?
- Who else is seeing things I'm not seeing?

- What assumptions am I making about "how things work" that may no longer be valid?

EAST: ASSESSMENT - EVALUATE OPTIONS

Once you understand the context, you need to assess your options. This isn't about finding the "perfect" solution, it's about identifying viable paths forward given current constraints and opportunities.

Assessment requires honest evaluation of:

What's Working: Which current approaches are still effective? What should we preserve and protect? Where are we seeing positive momentum?

What's Not Working: Which strategies are no longer effective? What's consuming resources without producing results? Where are we stuck in legacy thinking?

What's Possible: Given current reality, what opportunities exist? What new approaches might work? Who or what could we partner with? What constraints could become catalysts?

What's Non-Negotiable: What values, mission elements, or commitments must be preserved regardless of circumstances? What lines won't we cross even under pressure?

The best assessments involve diverse perspectives. In 2008, I convened cross-functional teams to evaluate our options. Technical staff saw possibilities I missed. Budget analysts identified constraints I hadn't considered. Program managers surfaced concerns about implementation. The collective assessment was far richer than what I could have produced alone.

Assessment tools:

- SWOT analysis (Strengths, Weaknesses, Opportunities, Threats)
- Scenario planning (best case, worst case, most likely case)
- Decision matrices (evaluate options against weighted criteria)

- Pre-mortem analysis (imagine the decision failed why?)
- Stakeholder mapping (who's affected and how?)

South: Adjustment - Make Strategic Pivots

This is where many leaders struggle actually making the changes that assessment reveals are necessary. We get attached to our original plans. We're invested in strategies we've already announced. We're reluctant to admit that what we thought would work isn't working.

Stephen Covey teaches that effective people are proactive they act based on values and conscious choice, not just reacting to circumstances (Habit 1). Adjustment is proactive adaptation. It's choosing to change your approach based on new information rather than stubbornly sticking with a plan that no longer serves your purpose.

Strategic adjustment requires three types of flexibility:

1. Tactical Flexibility: Changing your methods while keeping your goals constant. This is the most common type of adaptation you're still heading north, but you're taking a different route.

Example: During the financial crisis, we kept our goal of modernizing state IT infrastructure but shifted from capital-intensive hardware purchases to operational cloud services.

2. Strategic Flexibility: Changing your goals to align with new realities while staying true to your mission. The destination shifts, but the purpose remains.

Example: When I transitioned from government to private sector airport concessions, my mission of service and development remained constant, but my strategic goals shifted from policy implementation to operational excellence and business development.

3. Structural Flexibility: Changing how you organize resource, and operate to enable new strategies. This is the deepest form of

adaptation you're restructuring the foundation to support different approaches.

Example: Creating cross-functional teams instead of siloed departments, implementing agile methodologies instead of waterfall processes, or shifting from hierarchical to distributed decision-making.

The key to successful adjustment is communicating the "why" clearly. When you pivot, your team needs to understand that this isn't random, it's a thoughtful response to changed conditions. Use the CLEAR Communication Model from Chapter 3 to frame the adjustment, engage input, and align on the new direction.

Questions for making adjustments:

- What am I holding onto that I need to let go of?
- What's the smallest change that could produce the biggest impact?
- Who will be most affected by this adjustment and how can I support them?
- Am I adjusting out of fear or out of strategic thinking?

WEST: ACTION - EXECUTE WITH AGILITY

The final point on the compass is where adaptation becomes real through action. But this isn't the same as the bold, confident action from the Confidence Cycle in Chapter 1. This is agile action moving forward decisively while remaining alert to new information that might require further adjustment.

Agile action has three characteristics:

1. Iterative: You don't wait for the perfect plan. You move in the right direction, learn from initial results, and adjust rapidly. Think "test and learn" rather than "plan and perfect."

2. Responsive: You stay attuned to feedback from your environment about customer reactions, team concerns, early results, competitive moves and incorporate that feedback quickly.

3. Resilient: When actions don't produce expected results, you maintain momentum rather than getting derailed. You treat setbacks as information, not failure.

Remember Les Brown's teaching: "It's not over until you win." Adaptable action means continuing to move forward, learning and adjusting, until you achieve your objective even if the path looks nothing like what you originally planned.

During the technology transformation, we implemented a "pilot, learn, scale" approach. Rather than rolling out massive changes all at once, we tested new cloud services with small departments, gathered data, refined the approach, then expanded. This agile action allowed us to catch problems early when stakes were low and amplify successes when they proved effective.

Keys to agile action:

- Start small, learn fast, scale what works
- Build feedback loops into every initiative
- Celebrate learning, not just success
- Give teams permission to adjust to the course without seeking approval
- Review and adjust regularly, not just at project end

The Mindset of Adaptability

The Adaptability Compass provides a process, but adaptability ultimately requires the right mindset. Over my career, I've identified five mental shifts that enable sustained adaptability:

MINDSET 1: EMBRACE UNCERTAINTY AS OPPORTUNITY

Most people view uncertainty as threatening it triggers anxiety and a desire to return to stability. But uncertainty also creates opportunities. When conditions are stable, competitive advantages are entrenched. When everything shifts, new possibilities emerge.

The 2008 financial crisis forced government technology leaders to question assumptions that had been true for decades. This disruption was painful, but it also accelerated innovation that might have taken ten years under normal conditions. Cloud computing, shared services, and agile development gained traction precisely because the old ways were no longer viable.

Practice: When facing uncertainty, ask yourself, "What opportunity might this create that didn't exist before?" Train your brain to scan for possibility, not just threat.

MINDSET 2: HOLD PLANS LOOSELY, PRINCIPLES FIRMLY

Many leaders get this backward they hold too tightly to their plans while being flexible about their principles. Adaptive leaders do the opposite.

Your principles, your values, your mission, your commitments to people these should be non-negotiable. But your plans should be hypotheses, subject to revision based on new information.

Throughout my career transitions from county to state government, from public to private sector, from operations to consulting my core principles remained constant: service, excellence, development, integrity, anticipation. But my plans changed dramatically based on context.

Practice: Write down your top 5 principles. Now review your current plans are any of them being treated as if they were principles. Where might you need to loosen your grip?

MINDSET 3: CULTIVATE BEGINNER'S MIND

Expertise can become a liability when conditions change. Your deep knowledge of "how things work" may be based on conditions that no longer exist. Zen Buddhism teaches the concept of "beginner's mind" approaching situations with openness and curiosity, even when you're experienced.

When I moved from government to airport concessions, I had to embrace beginner's mind. Much of my government leadership experience was relevant, but I couldn't assume I knew how commercial retail operations worked. I asked basic questions. I observed before prescribing. I learned from people at every level of the organization.

This humility rooted in self-awareness from Chapter 2 made my adaptation faster and more effective. I wasn't trying to force my old mental models onto a new context.

Practice: When entering unfamiliar situations, explicitly tell yourself, "I'm a beginner here." Ask "dumb questions." Resist the urge to prove your expertise.

MINDSET 4: BUILD RESILIENCE THROUGH RECOVERY PRACTICE

T.D. Jakes teaches that resilience isn't about avoiding difficulties, it's about recovering from them. You build resilience the same way you build muscle: through repeated cycles of stress and recovery.

Every time you face a setback, adapt, and move forward, you're strengthening your adaptability capacity. The first time a plan fails, it's devastating. The tenth time? You have a toolkit of recovery strategies.

I've learned to reframe setbacks as training: "This is building my resilience for the next challenge." That budget meeting that went poorly? It taught me invaluable lessons about communication. The technology project that initially struggled. It showed me how to pivot under pressure.

Practice: After setbacks, explicitly capture what you learned and how you recovered. Over time, you'll notice your recovery time shortening what used to derail you for weeks now only slows you for days.

MINDSET 5: STAY CONNECTED TO PURPOSE

The anchor point for all adaptation is purpose. *Why* you're leading matters more than *what* you're doing. When the what changes and it will the why keeps you grounded.

My purpose has always been to develop people and deliver value through service. That purpose has remained constant whether I was managing budgets in county government, leading technology transformation at the state level, or developing minority-owned businesses in airport concessions.

When conditions change and I need to adapt, I return to purpose: "How can I continue serving and developing people in this new context?" This question guides my adaptation and prevents me from losing myself in the chaos of change.

Practice: Clarify your leadership purpose in a single sentence. When facing necessary adaptations, ask, "How does this change help me fulfill my purpose?" If it doesn't, reconsider the adaptation.

Leading Others Through Change

Your personal adaptability is crucial, but as a leader, you also need to help others adapt. Change is inherently difficult for people, it triggers uncertainty, fear of loss, and resistance. How you lead through change determines whether your team thrives or fractures.

Here are five principles for leading adaptive teams:

1. Acknowledge the Loss

When things change, people lose something even if the change is positive. They lose familiar routines, established relationships, proven approaches, or simply the comfort of knowing what to expect. Don't minimize this loss. Acknowledge it explicitly: "I know this change means letting go of ways of working that have served us well. That's hard." This validation creates psychological safety for adaptation.

2. Paint the Destination, Not Just the Journey

People can handle uncertainty about the path if they're clear on the destination. Help them see what success looks like on the other side of change. Make it concrete and compelling. During the financial crisis, I couldn't promise when budgets would recover, but I could paint a vision of a leaner, more efficient, more innovative technology organization that would emerge stronger.

3. Involve People in the How

You might need to decide *that* change is necessary but engage your team in determining *how* to implement it. People resist imposed change but embrace change they help create. Use the CLEAR Communication Model listen to their concerns, engage their ideas, and align approaches together.

4. Create Quick Wins

Momentum matters during change. Identify initiatives that can produce visible results quickly within 30-60 days. These quick wins build confidence that the new approach is working and create positive energy for sustained effort. We prioritized high-impact, low-complexity cloud migrations early to demonstrate that the new model worked.

5. Model Adaptive Behavior

Your team takes cues from you. If you're anxious and rigid, they'll be anxious and rigid. If you're calm, curious, and flexible, they'll mirror that. Show them what adaptability looks like: admit when your plan isn't working, ask for input, adjust course publicly, celebrate learning from failures. Your behavior gives them permission to be adaptive too.

AI Applications: Enhancing Adaptability with Technology

AI can dramatically enhance your ability to read context, assess options, and adapt quickly. While human judgment remains essential, AI provides analytical capabilities and scenario planning that would take teams weeks to produce manually.

Here are five AI applications for adaptive leadership:

AI Tool 1: Environmental Scanning and Trend Analysis

Use AI to monitor your environment and identify emerging trends that require adaptation.

Sample AI Prompt:

"I lead [type of organization] in [industry/sector]. What are the top 5 external trends in the next 12-24 months that could significantly impact our operations? For each trend, describe: 1) What's changing and why, 2) How it might affect us specifically, 3) Whether this is temporary or permanent, 4) What adaptive responses we should consider. Focus on trends in: technology, regulation, market dynamics, competitive landscape, and workforce expectations."

This proactive scanning helps you anticipate needed adaptations before they become crises.

AI Tool 2: Scenario Planning and Strategic Options

Use AI to develop multiple scenarios and evaluate strategic options for each.

Sample AI Prompt:

"We're facing [specific change/challenge]. Help me develop three scenarios: 1) Best case if this develops favorably, 2) Worst case if this creates maximum disruption, 3) Most likely case realistic middle ground. For each scenario, identify strategic options available to us, resources required, risks and opportunities, timeline for decision-making. This structured analysis helps you prepare for multiple futures and make more informed adaptation decisions.

AI Tool 3: Change Impact Analyzer

Before implementing changes, use AI to analyze potential impacts across your organization.

Sample AI Prompt:

"We're planning to [describe planned change]. Analyze the impact on: 1) Day-to-day operations (what disruptions?), 2) Team dynamics (who's most affected?), 3) Stakeholders (who needs to be brought along?), 4) Resources (what's required?), 5) Timeline (what's realistic?), 6) Risk factors (what could go wrong?). Identify the top 3 potential resistance points and recommend strategies to address them proactively."

This helps you anticipate challenges and plan more effective management strategies.

AI Tool 4: Adaptive Action Plan Generator

Use AI to create iterative action plans that build in flexibility and learning loops.

Sample AI Prompt:

"Create an adaptive action plan for [initiative/change]. Structure it with 1) Week 1-2: Quick wins and pilot tests, 2) Week 3-4: Learning review and adjustment, 3) Week 5-8: Scaled implementation with feedback loops, 4) Week 9-12: Full rollout and refinement. For each phase, specify key actions, success metrics, decision points for adjustment, and who's accountable. Build in explicit review moments where we can pivot based on learnings."

This creates plans that expect adaptation rather than rigid adherence to initial assumptions.

AI TOOL 5: RESILIENCE PATTERN RECOGNITION

Use AI to analyze your past adaptations and identify what works for you specifically.

Sample AI Prompt:

"I'm going to describe 3-5 times when I successfully

adapted to significant change. For each, I'll share: the situation, what I did, what worked, what didn't, and the outcome. Analyze these for patterns: 1) What adaptive strategies do I use consistently? 2) What conditions enable my best adaptation? 3) What barriers tend to slow me down? 4) What's my typical adaptation timeline? 5) Based on these patterns, what specific recommendations would help me adapt more effectively to [current challenge]?"

This self-knowledge helps you leverage your natural adaptive strengths and compensate for blind spots.

Reflection Questions

Use these questions to assess your adaptability and identify areas for growth.

- When I think about the last significant change I faced, how quickly did I move through the Adaptability Compass (Context → Assessment → Adjustment → Action)? Where did I get stuck?
- Am I holding any plans too tightly that should be flexible? Am I flexible about any principles that should be non-negotiable?
- How do I typically respond to uncertainty as threat or

opportunity? What would shift if I trained myself to see possibility first?

- What's one area where my expertise might be blinding me to new realities? Where do I need to cultivate beginner's mind?
- How am I helping my team adapt to current changes? Which of the five principles (acknowledge loss, paint destination, involve in how, create wins, model behavior) needs more attention?
- When I look at the trends shaping my industry/sector, what adaptations will likely be required in the next 12-24 months? Am I preparing proactively or waiting reactively?

Action Steps: Building Your Adaptability This Week

Adaptability is a skill you develop through practice. Choose at least two action steps to implement immediately.

Action Step 1: Map Your Current Context

Spend 30 minutes analyzing your current environment using the three context dimensions: External (market, competition, trends), Internal (culture, capability, resources), and Temporal (where you are in the cycle, what season you're in). Write down what's actually changing vs. what feels like it's changing. Identify one adaptation this analysis suggests you should make.

Action Step 2: Practice Letting Go

Identify one plan, process, or approach you're holding onto that no longer serves your purpose. Schedule time this week to officially "sunset" it communicate the change, transition to a new approach, and close the loop. Notice the emotions this brings up and practice moving through them.

ACTION STEP 3: CONDUCT A PRINCIPLES AUDIT

Write down your core leadership principles, the non-negotiables that guide all your decisions. Now review your calendar and decisions from last month. Are your actions aligned with these principles? Where is there a gap? What adjustment would better honor your principles?

ACTION STEP 4: CREATE AN ADAPTIVE ACTION PLAN

Take a current initiative and restructure it using iterative cycles: pilot (2 weeks), learn and adjust (1 week), scale (4 weeks), review and refine (1 week). Build in explicit decision points where you'll evaluate whether to continue, adjust, or stop. Share this approach with your team and explain why you're building in flexibility.

ACTION STEP 5: HAVE A RESILIENCE CONVERSATION

Sit down with your team and discuss how you collectively handle change. Ask: What helps us adapt well? What gets in our way? How can we support each other better during transitions? What would make us more resilient as a team? Use their input to co-create team norms for adaptive behavior.

Chapter Summary: Key Takeaways

- Adaptability is a survival requirement for leaders. The ability to read changing conditions, let go of what's not working, and pivot to new approaches determines long-term success.
- The Adaptability Compass provides four directional points: Context (read the environment), Assessment (evaluate options), Adjustment (make strategic pivots), Action (execute with agility).

- Leadership is a fluid process, not a fixed state. Like water adapting to its container, effective leaders adjust their approach based on changing conditions while staying true to core purpose.
- Five mindsets enable sustained adaptability: embrace uncertainty as opportunity, hold plans loosely and principles firmly, cultivate beginner's mind, build resilience through recovery practice, stay connected to purpose.
- Agile action is iterative, responsive, and resilient. Test and learn rather than plan and perfect. Stay attuned to feedback and adjust rapidly.
- Leading others through change requires: acknowledging loss, painting the destination, involving people in the how, creating quick wins, and modeling adaptive behavior.
- Resilience comes from repeated cycles of stress and recovery. Each adaptation strengthens your capacity for the next one. Reframe setbacks as training.
- AI can enhance adaptability through environmental scanning, scenario planning, change impact analysis, adaptive action planning, and resilience pattern recognition.

Les Brown teaches, "It's not over until you win." Adaptability is how you keep moving forward learning, adjusting, persisting until you achieve your objective, even when the path looks nothing like what you originally planned.

You've now completed Part I: Foundation Leading Yourself First. You've built authentic confidence, developed deep self-awareness, mastered high-performance communication, and learned to adapt in changing environments. These capabilities form the foundation for everything that follows.

In Part II, we shift focus from leading yourself to Leading Others Building High-Performance Teams. Chapter 5 begins with perhaps the most important transition in any leader's journey: From Boss to Leader.

The strongest leaders aren't the most rigid. They're the most fluid.

PART II

LEADING OTHERS - BUILDING HIGH-PERFORMANCE TEAMS

- *Chapter 5: From Boss to Leader*
- *Chapter 6: Developing and Mentoring Others*
- *Chapter 7: Strategic Thinking and Anticipating Needs*
- *Chapter 8: Leading Through Crisis*

Chapter 5

From Boss to Leader

"Leadership is influence nothing more, nothing less."

John C. Maxwell

The Title Didn't Make Me a Leader

When I became Chief Administrative Officer for the county government early in my career, I was excited. The title felt significant. The authority was real. I had a team, a budget, and the power to make decisions that affected thousands of people.

I thought the position made me a leader.

But within my first few weeks, I learned a humbling lesson: A title can make you a boss, but it doesn't make you a leader.

I discovered this when I tried to implement a new process for budget approvals. It was a good process, more efficient, more transparent, better aligned with best practices. I announced the change at a staff meeting, explained the rationale, and expected compliance.

What I got was resistance. Not overt defiance people were too professional for that but passive resistance. The new process was "tried" but somehow never quite implemented. Old habits persisted. Workarounds emerged. Progress stalled.

I was frustrated. I had the authority to require this change. Why wasn't it happening?

A veteran department director pulled me aside after a particularly tense meeting. "Major," he said carefully, "you have a good idea. But you're trying to force it rather than lead us to it. We don't resist the process we resist being told what to do without being part of creating the solution."

That conversation changed my leadership trajectory.

I called another meeting but this time, I came with questions, not answers. "What problems are you seeing with our current budget process?" I asked. "If you could design an ideal system, what would it look like?" "What concerns do you have about making changes?"

The conversation was rich. People shared insights I hadn't considered. They identified problems I hadn't seen. And together *together* we designed a process that was actually better than my original proposal.

More importantly, they owned it. Because they helped create it, they were invested in making it work. Implementation was smooth. Adoption was quick. The change stuck.

This experience taught me John Maxwell's foundational principle: Leadership is influence, not position. You can have authority without influence that makes you a boss. But influence without authority? That makes you a leader.

The Critical Distinction: Boss vs. Leader

The transition from boss to leader is one of the most important and most difficult evolutions in a career. Many people get promoted into management positions and remain bosses their entire careers. They rely on positional authority to get things done. They command compliance but never inspire commitment.

True leaders transcend their titles. They influence people who don't report to them. They create followership that persists even when they change roles. They make people feel valued rather than managed.

John Maxwell teaches that there are five levels of leadership:

Level 1 - Position: People follow because they have to

Level 2 - Permission: People follow because they want to

Level 3 - Production: People follow because of what you've accomplished

Level 4 - People Development: People follow because of what you've done for them

Level 5 - Pinnacle: People follow because of who you are and what you represent

Most people get stuck at Level 1. They have a title and they use it. But bosses operate at Level 1. Leaders climb to Level 2 and beyond.

Here's the practical difference:

A boss says: "Do this because I'm in charge."

A leader says: "Let me show you why this matters and how we can accomplish it together."

A boss asks: "Did you do what I told you?"

A leader asks: "What obstacles are you facing? How can I help?"

A boss thinks: "My job is to direct and control."

A leader thinks: "My job is to develop and empower."

A boss measures success by: "Did people do what I said?"

A leader measures success by: "Did we achieve the outcome? Did people grow in the process?"

The shift from boss to leader requires letting go of control in exchange for influence. It's counterintuitive when you get authority, the instinct is to use it. But the most effective leaders use their authority sparingly and rely instead on influence, relationship, and trust.

Framework: The Leadership Transition Matrix

Moving from boss to leader isn't a single event, it's a series of intentional transitions across four dimensions. I call this the Leadership Transition Matrix. Each dimension represents a fundamental shift in how you think about and practice leadership.

The four transitions are:

Transition 1: From Directing to Developing

Bosses direct. Leaders develop.

When you're a boss, you see your role as telling people what to do and ensuring they do it. Your mental model is: I have expertise, they need direction, I provide it. This works for simple, short-term tasks. But it creates dependency, stifles initiative, and limits your team's capacity to what you personally can oversee.

When you're a leader, you see your role as developing people's capability to solve problems independently. Your mental model is: They have potential, I create conditions for growth, they become more capable. This takes longer initially but multiplies your impact exponentially.

Throughout my career, from county government to Chief of Staff to running Great Foods LLC I've learned that my most lasting impact comes from the people I developed, not the problems I solved. That saying "Once you work for Major, you always work for Major" reflects this transition. I invested in developing people, and they became capable leaders themselves.

How to make this transition:

- Replace "Here's what to do" with "What do you think we should do?"
- When people bring you problems, resist solving them immediately. Ask: "What solutions have you considered?" "What would you do if I weren't available?" "What do you need from me to move forward?"
- Give assignments that stretch people just beyond their current capability not so far, they fail, but far enough they grow
- Debrief both successes and failures with learning questions: "What did you learn?" "What would you do differently next time?" "How did this challenge develop your skills?"

- Measure your success not by how many problems you solved, but by how many problem-solvers you created

Transition 2: From Controlling to Empowering

Bosses control. Leaders empower.

Control feels safe. When you control decisions, information, and resources, you can ensure things are done your way. The problem? Control has a limited radius. You can only control what you can directly oversee, which caps your organization's effectiveness at your personal bandwidth.

Empowerment feels risky. When you empower people to make decisions, you give up control. They might choose differently than you would. They might make mistakes. But empowerment has unlimited radius it scales through every person who has authority to act.

During my tenure as Chief of Staff, the longest-serving in Maryland history I couldn't possibly control every decision across the entire state government apparatus. I had to empower department heads, deputies, and team members to act with delegated authority. My role wasn't to make every decision; it was to ensure people had clarity about their authority, alignment with our objectives, and support when they needed it.

The key to empowerment is creating clear boundaries within which people have freedom:

Clear Outcomes: Define what success looks like, not how to achieve it

Clear Constraints: Specify non-negotiables (budget limits, legal requirements, core values)

Clear Authority: Be explicit about what they can decide independently vs. what requires consultation

Clear Support: Make yourself available when they need guidance, but don't hover

Within these boundaries, you give people room to choose their approach, make decisions, and learn from consequences. This requires trusting that they'll make reasonable choices and being willing to support them even when they choose differently than you would have.

How to make this transition:

- Identify decisions you're making that others could make. Start delegating them with clear boundaries.
- When people ask for approval, ask instead: "What do you recommend?" Then support their recommendation unless there's a compelling reason not to.
- Create a decision-making framework: "You decide" (full authority), "Decide and inform" (decide but tell me), "Recommend" (propose for approval), "Input" (I'll decide but want your perspective)
- When mistakes happen, focus on learning, not punishment: "What did we learn?" not "Who's to blame?"
- Publicly support decisions made by your team, even if you would have chosen differently (as long as they're within boundaries and reasonable)

Transition 3: From Telling to Asking

Bosses tell. Leaders ask.

This transition was difficult for me. I was good at solving problems. I could quickly assess situations and identify solutions. When people brought me challenges, my instinct was to tell them what to do. It was efficient problem presented, solution provided, conversation over.

But efficiency isn't the same as effectiveness. When you tell people what to do, you solve this problem but don't build their capability to solve the next one. When you ask questions that prompt their thinking, you take longer now but build problem-solving capacity for the future.

Stephen Covey's Habit 5 Seek first to understand, then to be understood applies here. Before telling people your solution, ask questions to understand their perspective:

- "What's your analysis of the situation?"
- "What options have you considered?"
- "What would success look like?"
- "What's your recommendation and why?"
- "What support do you need from me?"

Often, through this questioning process, people arrive at solutions as good or better than what you would have prescribed. And because they developed it themselves, they own it more fully.

There are still times when telling is appropriate in crises, with new employees who lack context, or when you have information, they don't. But make asking your default and telling your exception.

The coaching ratio: Aim for 80% questions, 20% statements

when developing people. Reverse that ratio only when immediate action is required.

How to make this transition:

- Practice pausing before answering. When someone asks your opinion, ask a question first: "What do you think?"
- Prepare a set of go-to coaching questions you can deploy in any situation
- When you do provide directions, explain your thinking: "Here's why I'm suggesting this..." rather than just "Do this."
- Resist the urge to rescue people from challenges too quickly. Struggle builds capability.
- After providing input, check for understanding and invite their perspective: "Does that make sense? What's your reaction?"

Transition 4: From Managing Work to Leading People

Bosses manage work. Leaders lead people.

This is perhaps the most fundamental shift. When you're focused on managing work, your attention is on tasks, deadlines, processes, and outputs. You see people as resources to accomplish the work.

When you're focused on leading people, your attention is on growth, motivation, relationships, and development. You see work as a vehicle for people to grow and contribute meaningfully.

The distinction matters because people can tell which you prioritize. When they sense you care more about the work than about them, they disengage. When they sense you care about *them* and their growth, they give discretionary effort.

T.D. Jakes teaches that authentic leadership requires genuinely valuing and empowering others. This isn't manipulation "I'll pretend to care so they'll work harder." It's genuine investment in people's success and wellbeing because they matter as humans, not just as contributors to organizational goals.

My core principle has always been service leadership is about serving others, not being served. This means putting people first, even when it's inconvenient. It means protecting their time, advocating for their development, celebrating their wins, and supporting them through challenges.

Leading people means:

- Knowing what matters to each person beyond work, their goals, families, interests, concerns
- Connecting work assignments to individual development goals
- Investing time in one-on-one conversations focused on their growth, not just task status
- Making people feel genuinely valued and important (which ties back to my core leadership approach)
- Creating psychological safety where people can take risks, make mistakes, and learn
- Advocating for people's careers even when it means they might leave your team for better opportunities

The irony is that when you lead people well, the work takes care of itself. Engaged, developed, valued people produce exceptional results not because you're managing every detail, but because they're invested in the mission and their own growth.

How to make this transition:

- Schedule regular one-on-ones with each team member, and protect that time
- Start meetings by asking how people are doing and actually listen to the answer
- Create individual development plans with each person, focusing on their career aspirations
- Celebrate people publicly and specifically not just "good job" but "here's specifically what you did well and why it mattered"
- When someone is struggling, ask "How can I support you?" before asking "When will this be done?"
- Remember birthdays, work anniversaries, and personal milestones, small gestures that show people matter

The Test of True Leadership

How do you know if you've successfully made the transition from boss to leader? John Maxwell offers a simple test: Do people follow you because they have to or because they want to?

Here are five indicators that you've become a leader, not just a boss:

INDICATOR 1: PEOPLE BRING YOU THEIR BEST IDEAS, NOT JUST THEIR PROBLEMS

When people see you as a boss, they bring you problems

because you have authority to fix them. When they see you as a leader, they bring you opportunities because they trust you'll help them develop their ideas. They're excited to share innovations, not just seeking permission or rescue.

Indicator 2: Your Influence Extends Beyond Your Direct Reports

Bosses can only influence people who report to them. Leaders influence peers, people in other departments, and even those senior to them. If people who don't work for you seek your input and value your perspective, you're leading, not just managing.

Indicator 3: People Grow Under Your Leadership

Look at the people who've worked for you. Did they get promoted? Did they develop new capabilities? Did they become leaders themselves? If your team members consistently advance in their careers, you're developing them, not just using them. My legacy of "Once you work for Major, you always work for Major" reflects this people grew under my leadership and continued to thrive afterward.

Indicator 4: Your Team Performs Well Even When You're Not Present

If work only gets done when you're directing it, you're a boss. If your team continues to excel when you're away making good decisions, solving problems, maintaining standards you've created a culture of empowerment and ownership. True leaders make themselves optional for day-to-day excellence.

INDICATOR 5: PEOPLE CHOOSE TO STAY CONNECTED AFTER REPORTING STRUCTURE CHANGES

When you change roles or people leave your team, do they maintain the relationship? Do they continue to seek your counsel? Do they stay in touch because they valued you as a person, not just as a boss? Lasting relationships beyond formal reporting structures are the truest measure of leadership impact.

AI Applications: Accelerating the Boss-to-Leader Transition

AI can help you make the transition from boss to leader by providing coaching, feedback analysis, and development planning capabilities that would traditionally require external consultants or extensive personal reflection.

Here are five AI applications for becoming a better leader:

AI TOOL 1: LEADERSHIP STYLE SELF-ASSESSMENT

Use AI to assess where you currently operate on the boss-to-leader spectrum.

Sample AI Prompt:

"I'm going to describe how I typically handle situations with my team. For each, tell me whether I'm operating as a 'boss' (relying on position) or a 'leader' (building influence), and provide specific recommendations for shifting toward leadership. Situations: 1) How I assign work, 2) How I handle mistakes, 3) How I make decisions, 4) How I develop people, 5) How I communicate expectations. Here's my current approach to each: [describe your approaches]. Where am I stuck in 'boss' mode and how can I transition to 'leader' mode?"

This creates awareness of specific patterns you need to change.

AI Tool 2: Coaching Question Generator

Build your repertoire of coaching questions for common situations.

Sample AI Prompt:

"Generate 5-7 powerful coaching questions I can use for each of these situations: 1) Team members bring me a problem, 2) Someone asks for my decision on their proposal, 3) Project isn't going well, 4) Person is struggling with a skill gap, 5) Team member has a conflict with a peer. For each situation, provide questions that will prompt their thinking rather than me providing answers. Make the questions open-ended and development focused."

Keep these questions readily available for quick reference during coaching moments.

AI Tool 3: Delegation Decision Framework

Use AI to help you identify what to delegate and how to empower effectively.

Sample AI Prompt:

"I currently handle the following decisions and tasks: [list your current responsibilities]. Help me identify: 1) Which decisions/tasks I should fully delegate with 'decide and inform' authority, 2) Which should be delegated with 'recommend for approval', 3) Which should keep making but with team input, 4) Which I must retain. For each delegation recommendation, provide: who's best suited, what boundaries to set, how to support them, and how to track without micromanaging."

This helps you strategically empower your team while maintaining appropriate oversight.

AI Tool 4: Individual Development Plan Creator

Create personalized development plans that demonstrate you're investing in people, not just managing work.

Sample AI Prompt:

"Help me create a development plan for a team member with this profile: Current role: [role], Current strengths: [strengths], Development areas: [areas], Career aspirations: [goals], Learning style: [preferences]. Create a 6-month plan including: specific skill-building activities, stretch assignments, learning resources, coaching focus areas, and successful metrics. Make it actionable and aligned with both their growth and our team's needs."

Personalized development plans show you care about people's growth beyond current job performance.

AI Tool 5: Leadership Communication Analyzer

Analyze your communication patterns to identify boss-like vs. leader-like language.

Sample AI Prompt:

"Analyze these recent emails/messages I sent to my team: [paste 5-10 communications]. Identify: 1) Language patterns that sound like 'boss' (directing, controlling, telling), 2) Language patterns that sound like 'leader' (developing, empowering, asking), 3) Specific phrases I overuse that undermine leadership,

4) Better alternatives that build influence rather than relying on authority. Provide before/after examples for each communication."

This reveals unconscious patterns in how you communicate and interact with your team.

Reflection Questions

These questions help you assess your progress from boss to leader.

- If my title were taken away tomorrow, how many people on my team would continue following my leadership? Why or why not?
- When was the last time I asked a coaching question instead of providing a direct answer? What stops me from asking more often?
- Do my team members bring me opportunities and ideas, or just problems and requests for decisions? What does this tell me about my leadership?
- Which of the four transitions (directing to developing, controlling to empowering, telling to asking, managing work to leading people) is hardest for me? Why?
- Can I name specific examples of how each team member has grown in the past year under my leadership? If not, what does that reveal?
- When people leave my team or I change roles, do they maintain the relationship? What does this say about whether I've been a boss or a leader?

Action Steps: Making the Transition This Week

The boss-to-leader transition requires intentional practice. Choose at least two action steps to implement immediately.

Action Step 1: Replace One 'Tell' with Five 'Asks'

For the next week, every time you're about to tell someone what to do, pause and ask a coaching question instead. Track how many times you successfully shift from telling to asking. Notice how it changes the conversation and the outcomes. Prepare 3-5 go-to coaching questions you can deploy in any situation.

Action Step 2: Delegate One Significant Decision

Identify one decision you currently make that someone

on your team could make with appropriate boundaries. Set clear outcomes, constraints, and authority level. Then let them make the decision and support it publicly, even if they choose differently than you would have. Debrief afterward to capture learning.

Action Step 3: Create Individual Development Plans

Schedule one-on-ones with each team member specifically to discuss their career aspirations and development goals. Don't talk about current projects focus entirely on where they want to grow. Then create concrete development plans with specific actions you'll take to support their growth. Follow through on these commitments.

Action Step 4: Audit Your Language

Review your last 10 emails or messages to your team.

Highlight every instance of boss language ("you need to," "make sure you," "I decided") vs. leader language ("what do you think," "how can I support," "I trust your judgment"). Set a goal to shift your ratio from boss to leader language. Rewrite three boss-style messages in leader style.

Action Step 5: Build Influence Beyond Your Team

Identify three people who don't report to you (peers, other departments, or senior leaders) and look for ways to add value to their work without any expectation of return. Share insights, make introductions, offer support. True leadership is measured by influence beyond positional authority.

Chapter Summary: Key Takeaways

- Leadership is influence, not position. A title can make you a boss, but only influence makes you a leader. The most effective leaders transcend their titles.
- Bosses rely on positional authority; leaders build influence through relationships, development, and trust. Position gets compliance; influence gets commitment.
- The Leadership Transition Matrix has four dimensions: directing to developing, controlling to empowering, telling to asking, and managing work to leading people.
- Developing people creates multiplied impact. When you develop problem-solvers instead of solving every problem yourself, your capacity becomes unlimited.
- Empowerment requires clear boundaries (outcomes, constraints, authority, support) within which people have freedom to choose their approach and make decisions.

- Asking coaching questions builds capability; telling provides answers but limits growth. Make asking your default and telling your exception.
- Leading people means genuinely caring about their growth, wellbeing, and success not just their contribution to organizational goals. People can tell the difference.
- Five tests of true leadership: people bring you ideas not just problems, your influence extends beyond direct reports, people grow under your leadership, your team performs well without you present, and relationships persist beyond reporting structures.
- AI can accelerate the boss-to-leader transition through self-assessment, coaching question generation, delegation frameworks, development planning, and communication analysis.

John Maxwell is right: leadership is influence nothing more, nothing less. Your title might open doors, but your influence determines what happens once you're inside. The transition from boss to leader is the difference between getting people to work for you and inspiring them to work with you toward something meaningful.

In the next chapter, we'll explore how to use your leadership influence to develop others systematically turning good performers into exceptional leaders through intentional mentoring and coaching.

Authority is what you have. Influence is what you earn. Leadership is the difference.

CHAPTER 6

DEVELOPING & MENTORING OTHERS

"You don't have to be great to get started,

but you have to get started to be great."

Les Brown

The Person Who Didn't Think They Could

Early in my tenure as Chief of Staff to the Governor, I had a mid-level analyst on our team let's call her Sarah who was technically competent but lacked confidence in her strategic thinking. She was excellent at executing assigned tasks but hesitant to offer ideas or challenge assumptions.

During a budget crisis meeting, I noticed Sarah had insights that weren't being heard. She would start to speak, then defer to more senior voices. She had the analysis, but not the confidence to assert it.

After that meeting, I pulled her aside. "Sarah, I noticed you had something to say about the revenue projections. What was it?"

She hesitated. "It's probably nothing. I'm sure the senior analysts already considered it."

"Tell me anyway," I said.

What she shared was a brilliant pattern in the data that others had missed, with significant implications for our budget planning. I asked her to develop a brief analysis. The next day, when she presented it, I made sure to publicly acknowledge her insight and its impact on our strategy.

But I didn't stop there. Over the following months, I intentionally created opportunities for Sarah to contribute at higher levels. I asked her to lead analysis on complex issues. I invited her to meetings where she could learn from senior leaders. I gave her feedback that was honest but focused on growth. When she succeeded, I made sure others knew. When she struggled, I coached her privately through the challenges.

I also did something crucial: I made her feel important. Not in a patronizing way, but by genuinely valuing her contributions and treating her insights with the same respect I gave to senior advisors. This is central to my leadership approach making people feel that their work matters, that *they* matter.

Within a year, Sarah was promoted to a senior analyst position. Within three years, she was leading her own team. Today, more than two decades later, she's a senior executive in state government. And when we reconnect, she still references that initial conversation and the development opportunities that followed as pivotal in her career.

This story captures the essence of development: seeing potential that people don't yet see in themselves, creating conditions for growth, coaching them to exceed their own expectations, and making them feel valued in the process.

Your Greatest Legacy: The People You Develop

John Maxwell teaches that Level 4 leadership People Development is where your influence multiplies exponentially. At this level, people follow you not just because of what you've accomplished (Level 3), but because of what you've done *for them.*

Over four decades of leadership, I've learned this truth: Your greatest accomplishments will be forgotten. The problems you solved will be replaced by new problems. The initiatives you launched will evolve beyond recognition. But the people you developed? They'll carry your influence forward for decades.

That's why I'm most proud of the legacy captured in that phrase: "Once you work for Major, you always work for Major." It's said with fondness, not obligation. People stay connected because the relationship was developmental, not transactional. They grew under my leadership, and they know I continue to invest in their success even years later.

T.D. Jakes emphasizes that empowering others is central to authentic leadership. When you genuinely invest in people's growth not for what they can do for you, but because you believe in their potential you create a ripple effect that extends far beyond your direct influence.

Consider this: Every person you develop goes on to lead others. If you develop 10 people who each develop 10 people, you've influenced 100 people you'll never meet. That's the multiplication of Level 4 leadership.

Development isn't a nice-to-have leadership activity. It's the *core* of sustainable leadership. Organizations that systematically develop people outperform, out-innovate, and outlast those that don't. Leaders who invest in development create loyalty, engagement, and results that far exceed what they could accomplish alone.

FRAMEWORK: THE DEVELOPMENT PIPELINE

Developing people isn't random or haphazard it follows a systematic process. I call this the Development Pipeline because it moves people through progressive stages of growth, just like a pipeline moves resources through successive phases of refinement.

The Development Pipeline has five stages:

IDENTIFY → INVEST → STRETCH → SUPPORT → RELEASE

STAGE 1: IDENTIFY - SEE POTENTIAL OTHERS DON'T

Development begins with recognition. You must see potential in people that they may not see in themselves. This requires looking beyond current performance to underlying capability, drive, and character.

Les Brown's principle applies here: "You don't have to be great to get started, but you have to get started to be great."

Many people with tremendous potential are waiting for someone to see it and believe in them. Your job as a leader is to be that someone.

What to look for when identifying high-potential people:

Curiosity: Do they ask insightful questions? Do they seek to understand beyond their immediate responsibilities? Curious people learn faster and adapt better.

Initiative: Do they see problems and address them without being asked? Do they volunteer for challenging assignments? Initiative signals someone ready for more responsibility.

Coachability: How do they respond to feedback? Do they implement suggestions? Can they take criticism without becoming defensive? The most talented person who won't be coached has limited growth potential.

Impact: Even in entry-level roles, do they create disproportionate value? Do they make things better wherever they are? High-impact performers at any level deserve development investment.

Character: Do they demonstrate integrity, even when it's costly? Do they treat everyone with respect? Do they own their mistakes? Character determines how far someone's talent can take them.

With Sarah, I identified potential because she combined deep analytical capability with genuine curiosity and strong character. Her lack of confidence was a development opportunity, not a disqualifier. In fact, talented people with humility often have higher development ceilings than arrogant high performers.

How to implement:

- Create a simple assessment: Rate each team member on curiosity, initiative, coachability, impact, and character (1-5 scale)
- Watch for people who consistently exceed expectations in their current role
- Pay attention to who asks the best questions in meetings
- Notice who others naturally turn to for help or advice
- Don't limit development to people you personally like focus on potential and character

STAGE 2: INVEST - COMMIT TIME AND ATTENTION

Once you've identified high-potential people, you must invest in them. Investment means dedicating your time, attention, and resources to their growth even when you're busy, even when it's inconvenient.

Many leaders say they value development but never create time for it. They're too focused on immediate deliverables to invest in long-term capability building. This is short-sighted. The time you invest in development today multiplies your capacity tomorrow.

Investment takes three forms:

1. Direct Time: Regular one-on-one meetings focused on their development, not just task updates. These should be sacred time protected, prepared for, and person-centered.

My practice: 60-minute development conversations monthly with each high-potential person. Agenda: their goals, current challenges, learning needs, feedback on recent work, coaching on specific skills. I prepare as seriously for these as I would for executive presentations.

2. Access and Exposure: Bringing people into settings where they can learn by observation and participation. This accelerates their understanding of organizational dynamics and strategic thinking.

Example: I brought Sarah to executive meetings where she initially had no formal role. I'd assign her to observe specific leaders or dynamics, then debrief afterward: "What did you notice about how the budget director framed that proposal? Why do you think it was effective?"

3. Advocacy: Using your influence to create opportunities for their visibility, advancement, and recognition. This includes recommending them for projects, introducing them to influential people, and publicly acknowledging their contributions.

Example: When Sarah's analysis proved valuable, I ensured the Governor knew whose work it was. When promotion opportunities arose, I advocated for her readiness even when others questioned whether she had enough experience.

Investment also means making people feel important and valued. This isn't about inflating egos it's about genuine appreciation for their contributions and potential. When people know you believe in them, they perform beyond what they thought possible.

How to implement:

- Block recurring time for development conversations and treat them as non-negotiable

- Intentionally include high-potential people in meetings above their current level
- Make introductions to people who can accelerate their learning or career
- Publicly credit their work and ideas, especially to senior leadership
- Track your time are you spending at least 20% on development? If not, something's wrong

STAGE 3: STRETCH - CREATE GROWTH THROUGH CHALLENGE

Investment creates the foundation, but growth happens through challenge. You must intentionally give people assignments that stretch them beyond their current capability not so far they fail catastrophically, but far enough that success requires new learning.

This is where many leaders fail at development. They either:

- Keep people in their comfort zones because "they're so good at this" (which prevents growth)
- Throw people into the deep end without support (which creates trauma, not development)

The right approach is supported stretch assignments that require growth, paired with coaching to navigate the challenges.

Stephen Covey's Habit 7 Sharpen the Saw applies here. You're helping people expand their capacity through progressive challenge. Each successful stretch builds confidence and capability for the next level of challenge.

Types of stretch assignments:

Complexity Stretch: Projects with more moving parts, stakeholders, or technical difficulty than they've handled before

Visibility Stretch: Presenting to senior leaders, representing the organization externally, or leading high-stakes initiatives

Authority Stretch: Leading teams, making decisions, managing budgets responsibilities that test their judgment and influence

Skill Stretch: Assignments that require developing new technical or functional expertise

Ambiguity Stretch: Challenges without clear solutions, requiring strategic thinking and creativity

With Sarah, I gave her increasingly complex analytical assignments, then had her present findings to progressively senior audiences. Each success built her confidence and capability. Each struggle and there were struggles became a coaching opportunity.

How to implement:

- Assess current capability, then assign work that's 10-20% beyond it
- Frame stretch assignments explicitly: "This will be challenging and you'll learn a lot. I'll support you."
- Check in regularly during stretch assignments don't just assign and disappear
- Make it safe to struggle normalize that growth involves temporary incompetence
- Debrief every stretch assignment: "What did you learn? What was hard? What will you do differently next time?"

STAGE 4: SUPPORT - COACH THROUGH THE STRUGGLE

Stretch without support is abandoned. As people navigate challenges beyond their current capability, they need coaching, encouragement, and sometimes intervention.

Support doesn't mean doing the work for them or rescuing them from every difficulty. It means providing the guidance and resources they need to succeed while allowing them to struggle enough to learn.

Effective support includes:

Real-Time Coaching: Brief, specific guidance at critical moments. Not lengthy development conversations just timely input when they need it most.

Example: Before Sarah's first presentation to the Governor's cabinet, I spent 15 minutes coaching her: "Focus on the recommendation first, then the supporting data. Make eye contact with the Governor when you state the key point. Expect pushback on the timeline here's how to respond."

Problem-Solving Partnership: When they're stuck, resist solving the problem for them. Instead, ask questions that guide their thinking: "What have you tried? What else could you try? Who else might have insight? What would success look like?"

Resource Provision: Connecting them with people, information, training, or tools they need to succeed. Sometimes support is simply removing barriers.

Emotional Support: Stretch assignments create anxiety and self-doubt. Part of support is believing in them when they doubt themselves, normalizing struggle as part of growth, and celebrating progress.

Strategic Intervention: Knowing when to step in and when to let them work it out. Step in when failure would be catastrophic or when they're truly in over their heads. Stay back when struggle is productive.

The art of support is calibrating how much to give based on the person and situation. New to the organization? More support. Proven track record in similar challenges? Less support. High stakes with little margin for error? More support. Learning opportunity with manageable risk? Less support.

How to implement:

- Schedule regular check-ins during stretch assignments, but let them drive the agenda
- Ask "What support do you need from me?" rather than assuming you know
- Make yourself available for brief coaching moments, not just scheduled meetings
- Connect them with others who can provide expertise or perspective you don't have
- Distinguish between "I'll show you how" (modeling), "Let's think through this together" (coaching), and "You've got this" (empowerment)

Stage 5: Release - Let Them Fly

The final stage of development is the hardest for many leaders: letting go. Release means allowing people to take on full authority and responsibility, trusting them to succeed without your constant involvement.

It also means supporting their advancement even when it means losing them from your team. True development-focused leaders celebrate when people outgrow their current roles and advocate for their promotion or new opportunities.

This is counterintuitive. You've invested significant time and energy developing someone. They're now performing at a high level. Your instinct might be to keep them they're too valuable to lose. But hoarding talent isn't leadership; it's selfishness.

Maxwell's Level 4 leaders understand this paradox: The more you release talented people to bigger opportunities; the more talented people want to work for you. Your reputation as a developer becomes a magnet for high-potential talent.

Release takes three forms:

Operational Release: Giving them full authority over decisions and outcomes in their domain. Moving from "Check with me before you decide" to "Use your judgment and keep me informed."

Career Release: Supporting their advancement into roles beyond your team, even to other organizations. Recommending them for opportunities, making introductions, and celebrating their success.

Relational Release: Transitioning from boss-subordinate to mentor-mentee or colleague-colleague relationships that continue beyond formal reporting structures. This is what creates "Once you work for Major, you always work for Major."

With Sarah, release meant recommending her for promotion even though it created a gap on my team. It meant celebrating her advancement publicly. And it meant maintaining our relationship as she continued to grow now as a peer and friend rather than as someone I managed.

How to implement:

- Explicitly expand authority as people demonstrate capability
- Have career conversations: "Where do you want to be in 3-5 years? How can I help you get there?"
- Actively recommend developed people for opportunities, even outside your organization
- Create succession plans that include promoting from within develop your own replacement
- Maintain relationships after people leave your team continue to mentor and support them

Five Principles of Effective Development

The Development Pipeline provides structure, but effective development also requires embracing key principles:

Principle 1: Develop the Whole Person, Not Just the Employee

T.D. Jakes emphasizes that authentic leadership means genuinely caring about people as individuals, not just as resources. When you develop someone, you're not just building a better employee you're helping a human being reach their potential.

This means understanding their aspirations beyond their current role, supporting their personal growth, and recognizing that professional development and personal development are interconnected.

Ask: What do they want to become, not just what do I need them to do?

Principle 2: Make Development Systematic, Not Random

Opportunistic development coaching people when you happen to think about it produces limited results. Systematic development creating structures, rhythms, and accountabilities creates sustainable growth.

This means scheduled development conversations, documented development plans, tracked progress, and regular assessment of whether your development efforts are working.

Principle 3: Customize Development to the Individual

One-size-fits-all development programs rarely work. People learn differently, are motivated by different things, and have different starting points. Effective development requires understanding each person's unique profile and tailoring your approach.

Some people need more encouragement; others need more challenges. Some learn best through doing, others through observation. Some need detailed guidance; others need space to figure things out.

Principle 4: Provide Honest Feedback, Not Just Encouragement

Development requires truth. If you only encourage and never

confront gaps, people don't grow. If you only criticize and never encourage, people become demoralized.

The balance is honest feedback delivered with genuine care. I coached Sarah on areas where she needed to grow her tendency to defer to others, her need to project more executive presence while also celebrating her analytical brilliance and growth mindset.

The formula: specific observations + impact + path forward, all wrapped in genuine belief in their potential.

Principle 5: Measure Success by Their Growth, Not Your Comfort

It's tempting to keep developed people in roles where they're comfortable and productive. But if someone has stopped growing, you've stopped developing them.

The measure of development success is whether people are consistently expanding their capabilities, taking on new challenges, and advancing toward their goals even if that creates disruption for you.

AI Applications: Accelerating People Development

AI can significantly enhance your ability to develop people systematically by helping you create personalized development plans, generate coaching questions, track progress, and identify patterns you might miss.

Here are five AI applications for effective development:

AI Tool 1: Personalized Development Plan Creator

Create comprehensive, individualized development plans

efficiently.

Sample AI Prompt:

"Create a 12-month development plan for: Current role: [role], Strengths: [list], Development areas: [list], Career aspirations: [goals], Learning preferences: [how they learn best]. Structure the plan across the Development Pipeline stages: Identify (skills to develop), Invest (time commitment and resources), Stretch (specific assignments), Support (coaching focus), Release (expanding authority). Include monthly milestones, learning activities, stretch assignments, and success metrics."

This creates a roadmap for development rather than hoping growth happens accidentally.

AI Tool 2: Coaching Conversation Guide

Prepare for development conversations with targeted questions and topics.

Sample AI Prompt:

"I'm having a development conversation with [person] who recently [specific situation/challenge]. Generate: 1) Opening questions to understand their perspective on what happened, 2) Coaching questions to prompt their thinking about how to handle it differently, 3) Feedback points I should raise (based on: [observations]), 4) Development actions we could commit to, 5) How to close the conversation with encouragement and clarity. Make questions open-ended and growth-focused."

This ensures development conversations are structured and productive, not rambling.

AI Tool 3: Stretch Assignment Matcher

Identify the right stretch assignments for each person's development needs.

Sample AI Prompt:

"I need to identify stretch assignments for team members with these profiles: [list 3-5 people with their current roles, strengths, and development goals]. We have these upcoming projects/opportunities: [list initiatives]. Match each person to assignments that would stretch them appropriately (10-20% beyond current capability). For each match, explain: why this stretch is appropriate, what they'll learn, what support they'll need, and how to set them up for success."

This helps you strategically deploy development opportunities rather than assigning work randomly.

AI Tool 4: Development Progress Tracker

Analyze development conversations and track progress over time.

Sample AI Prompt:

"I've been coaching [person] for 6 months. Here are notes from our development conversations: [paste notes from monthly meetings]. Analyze for: 1) Growth patterns where are they making consistent progress? 2) Stuck points where are they struggling repeatedly? 3) Commitment follow-through are they completing development actions we agree to? 4) Confidence trends are they becoming more/less confident? 5) Recommendations for adjusting my coaching approach or their development plan."

This reveals patterns you might miss in individual conversations and helps you adjust your approach.

AI TOOL 5: FEEDBACK FRAMING ASSISTANT

Craft constructive feedback that drives growth without creating defensiveness.

Sample AI Prompt:

"I need to give feedback to [person] about [specific behavior/situation]. Here's what I observed: [describe objectively]. Here's the impact: [consequences]. Help me frame this feedback using: 1) Specific observations (facts not judgments), 2) Impact explanation (why it matters), 3) Curiosity about their perspective ("Help me understand..."), 4) Collaborative problem-solving ("How might we..."), 5) Path forward (concrete next steps). Make it honest but encouraging, focusing on growth potential."

This helps you deliver difficult feedback in ways that maintain relationship while driving improvement.

Reflection Questions

Use these questions to assess your effectiveness as a developer of people.

- Can I name specific ways each person on my team has grown in the past year? If not, am I really developing them or just managing them?
- What percentage of my time goes to development versus operational management? Is that ratio what it should be given my role and impact?

- Do I have structured development plans for high-potential people, or am I hoping development happens organically? What's the difference in results?
- When was the last time I gave someone a genuine stretch assignment? Am I keeping people comfortable or pushing them to grow?
- Have I recommended anyone for promotion or new opportunities in the past year, even though it meant losing them from my team? What does my answer reveal?
- Do people who've worked for me maintain the relationship years later? Why or why not? What does this say about the depth of my development focus?

Action Steps: Becoming a Developer of People This Week

Development requires intentional action. Choose at least two action steps to implement immediately.

Action Step 1: Create Development Plans

Identify your top 3-5 high-potential team members. Schedule 90-minute conversations with each to discuss their career aspirations and create personalized development plans using the Development Pipeline framework. Document these plans and schedule quarterly reviews to track progress.

Action Step 2: Assign One Stretch Project

Identify someone ready for a stretch assignment. Give them a project that's 10-20% beyond their current capability. Frame it explicitly as a development opportunity, commit to supporting them through it, and schedule regular check-ins. Make it safe to struggle and learn.

ACTION STEP 3: BLOCK DEVELOPMENT TIME

Review your calendar and block recurring time for development activities: monthly one-on-ones with each high-potential person, preparation time before development conversations, and follow-through on development commitments. Treat this time as sacred development is your highest-leverage activity.

ACTION STEP 4: PRACTICE REAL-TIME COACHING

For the next week, whenever someone brings you a problem or asks for directions, pause and ask a coaching question before providing an answer: "What do you think we should do?" "What options have you considered?" "If you were making this decision, what would you choose?" Track how often you successfully shift from telling to coaching.

ACTION STEP 5: ADVOCATE FOR SOMEONE'S ADVANCEMENT

Identify one person ready for the next level. Actively advocate for their advancement, recommend them for a promotion, introduce them to senior leaders, nominate them for high-visibility projects, or help them explore opportunities outside your team. Practice releasing rather than hoarding talent.

Chapter Summary: Key Takeaways

- Your greatest legacy is the people you develop. Problems you solve will be forgotten, but people you grow will carry your influence forward for decades.
- The Development Pipeline has five stages: Identify (see potential), Invest (commit time and attention), Stretch (create growth through challenge), Support (coach through struggle), Release (let them fly).
- Look for five qualities when identifying high-potential people: curiosity, initiative, coachability, impact, and character. Talent without character has limited growth potential.
- Investment means dedicating time, providing access and exposure, and using your influence to advocate for people's growth. Making people feel important and valued is essential to development.
- Stretch assignments should extend people 10-20% beyond current capability enough to require growth, not so far they fail catastrophically. Supported stretch creates learning; unsupported stretch creates trauma.
- Support means coaching at critical moments, helping solve problems without solving them yourself, providing resources, offering emotional encouragement, and knowing when to step in versus when to let them struggle productively.
- Release means expanding authority, supporting advancement even when it means losing them, and maintaining relationships beyond formal reporting

structures. Hoarding talent isn't leadership it's selfishness.

- Five development principles: develop the whole person, make it systematic, customize to the individual, provide honest feedback with care, and measure success by their growth not your comfort.
- AI can accelerate development through personalized planning, coaching guides, stretch assignment matching, progress tracking, and feedback framing.

Les Brown teaches, "You don't have to be great to get started, but you have to get started to be great." As a developer of people, your job is to help them get started on their journey to greatness seeing potential they don't yet see in themselves, creating conditions for growth, and coaching them to exceed their own expectations.

In the next chapter, we'll explore Strategic Thinking & Anticipating Needs the capability that separates reactive managers from proactive leaders. Development creates capable people; strategic thinking ensures they're working on the right things.

The problems you solve will be forgotten. The people you develop will remember forever.

CHAPTER 7

STRATEGIC THINKING & ANTICIPATING NEEDS

"Begin with the end in mind."

Stephen R. Covey, Habit 2

The Budget Crisis That Never Happened

It was early in my tenure as Chief of Staff to Governor Glendening. During a routine review of state revenue projections, I noticed something that didn't sit right. The economic indicators looked solid on the surface unemployment was low, consumer spending was up, stock markets were climbing. But beneath those headlines, I saw subtle warning signs.

Manufacturing job losses in certain regions. Shifts in federal funding formulas that would hit us in 18 months. A cooling in the housing market that hadn't yet shown up in state revenue but would eventually. Tax collections that were meeting projections but not exceeding them the way they had in previous years.

Individually, none of these signals was alarming. Together, they suggested we might face a revenue shortfall within the next fiscal year not a crisis yet, but a headwind we needed to prepare for.

I brought this analysis to the Governor and budget director. The data didn't support immediate action we were still meeting projections. But I recommended we begin contingency planning: identify potential budget reductions, build reserves where possible, and delay non-essential spending commitments.

Some advisors thought I was being overly cautious. "Why cut now when we're hitting our numbers?" they asked. But the Governor trusted my instinct for anticipation we'd been through enough together that he knew when I flagged something, it was worth attention.

We implemented quiet preparation. Nothing dramatic just prudent positioning. We built contingency plans. We identified efficiencies. We had difficult but early conversations with agency heads about potential scenarios.

Fourteen months later, the revenue shortfall materialized. But unlike other states that faced sudden crisis, we were ready. We had options already developed. We had stakeholders already prepared. We had time to implement thoughtful solutions rather than making panic cuts.

While neighboring states made headlines with emergency budget sessions and drastic cuts, Maryland navigated the challenge smoothly. Nobody writes news stories about crises that don't happen. But that quiet success that's strategic thinking in action.

This story captures one of my core leadership principles: Anticipation. The best leaders don't just respond to what's happening they see what's coming and position themselves accordingly. They think several moves ahead, like chess masters, rather than reacting to the immediate situation.

The Difference Between Managing and Leading

Managers handle today. Leaders prepare for tomorrow.

This distinction is fundamental. Management is essential for organizations need people who can execute current operations effectively. But leadership requires something more: the ability to see beyond the immediate, to connect patterns others miss, and to position the organization for future success.

Stephen Covey's Habit 2 Begin with the End in Mind is about strategic thinking. Before you act, envision where you want to end up. Before you allocate resources, understand the outcomes you're pursuing. Before you commit to a path, consider where it leads.

Throughout my career; 40+ years across county government, state leadership as Chief of Staff, running Great Foods LLC for 20 years, and now consulting through Strategic Solutions Center I've found that *anticipation* is the differentiator between good leaders and great ones.

Consider how this played out across my career:

- As Chief Administrative Officer in county government, I anticipated infrastructure needs before they became crises, positioning us to secure funding when it became available

- As Chief of Staff, I anticipated political dynamics, budget pressures, and policy implications often seeing challenges months before they materialized
- During the 2008 financial crisis with Great Foods LLC, I anticipated that recovery would be slow and uneven, which shaped our operational strategy for sustainable survival rather than hoping for quick rebound
- As a consultant, I help clients anticipate industry trends, competitive threats, and organizational needs before they become urgent

Anticipation isn't about predicting the future with certainty that's impossible. It's about:

- Reading patterns and trends that indicate likely directions
- Thinking through implications and second-order effects
- Preparing for multiple scenarios rather than betting on one outcome
- Positioning yourself to respond effectively regardless of what actually happens
- Acting early when stakes are low rather than reacting late when options are limited

Framework: The Strategic Anticipation Cycle

Strategic thinking isn't a one-time exercise it's a continuous cycle of scanning, analyzing, positioning, and adjusting. I call this the Strategic Anticipation Cycle because it combines forward-thinking with proactive positioning.

THE CYCLE HAS FOUR PHASES:

SCAN → SYNTHESIZE → STRATEGIZE → STAGE

PHASE 1: SCAN - READ THE SIGNALS

Strategic thinking begins with environmental scanning systematically gathering information from diverse sources to understand what's happening in your environment and what might be emerging.

Most leaders scan too narrowly. They pay attention to their immediate industry or function but miss adjacent signals that will eventually affect them. Effective scanning requires deliberately widening your aperture.

What to scan:

Industry Trends: Technology shifts, regulatory changes, competitive moves, market dynamics, customer behavior patterns

Economic Indicators: Not just headline numbers but underlying patterns employment trends, investment flows, consumer confidence, supply chain dynamics

Political and Social Dynamics: Policy directions, public sentiment shifts, demographic changes, cultural trends

Organizational Health: Internal morale, capability gaps, process bottlenecks, cultural strengths and weaknesses

Adjacent Domains: Industries that touch yours, analogous situations in different contexts, innovations happening elsewhere that could apply to your work

When I was scanning revenue patterns as Chief of Staff, I wasn't just looking at state tax collections. I was reading federal economic reports, tracking regional employment data, monitoring housing market indicators, talking to business leaders about their hiring plans, and watching consumer spending patterns. Each source provided a piece of the picture.

How to scan effectively:

- Create a scanning routine dedicated time weekly to read, listen, and observe beyond your immediate work
- Diversify your information sources industry publications, general news, academic research, conversations with frontline staff, customer feedback, competitor analysis
- Look for weak signals small indicators that suggest larger trends before they're obvious
- Talk to people with different perspectives they see things you don't
- Ask "What's changing?" not just "What's happening?"

PHASE 2: SYNTHESIZE - CONNECT THE PATTERNS

Scanning produces information. Synthesis produces insight. This is where strategic thinking becomes art connecting disparate data points into coherent patterns that reveal what's likely to happen next.

Most people collect information but don't synthesize it. They know a lot of facts but can't see the story those facts tell. Strategic leaders ask: *What pattern is emerging here? What do these signals, taken together, suggest about the future?*

Synthesis involves:

Pattern Recognition: Identifying recurring themes across different data sources. When multiple indicators point in the same direction, that's a pattern worth attention.

Example: Individual indicators of manufacturing job losses, federal funding changes, and housing market cooling each meant little alone. Together, they formed a pattern suggesting economic headwinds that would affect state revenue.

Implication Mapping: Thinking through "if this, then what?" If this trend continues, what happens next? If this event occurs, who's affected and how?

Example: If housing markets cool, property tax revenue declines (direct impact) AND construction employment drops which reduces income tax revenue (secondary impact) AND consumer spending decreases which affects sales tax (tertiary impact).

Timeline Projection: Estimating when impacts will materialize. Some effects are immediate, others lag by months or years. Understanding timing helps you prepare appropriately.

Scenario Development: Creating multiple plausible futures based on how trends might develop. Not predicting THE future, but preparing for POSSIBLE futures.

Challenge Assumptions: Questioning your own synthesis. What am I missing? What assumptions am I making? What if I'm wrong? This prevents confirmation bias.

Tools for synthesis:

- Create a "strategic journal" where you note patterns you're seeing and update your thinking as new information arrives
- Use visual mapping draw connections between different trends and their implications
- Discuss emerging patterns with trusted advisors who will challenge your thinking
- Build multiple scenarios (best case, worst case, most likely case) to avoid anchoring on a single prediction
- Test your synthesis against past situations would this framework have predicted what actually happened?

PHASE 3: STRATEGIZE - DETERMINE YOUR RESPONSE

Once you understand what's likely coming, you need a strategy for how to respond. This is where anticipation converts to action planning.

Strategic response isn't about predicting exactly what will happen and betting everything on that prediction. It's about positioning yourself to succeed across multiple plausible scenarios.

Strategic response involves:

Define Success Outcomes: What does winning look like in each scenario? What are you trying to achieve or protect?

Example: In the revenue scenario, success meant avoiding service cuts, maintaining employee morale, and preserving strategic initiatives even if revenue declined.

Identify Strategic Options: What moves are available? What could you do proactively? What capabilities do you need? What partnerships might help?

Assess Trade-offs: Every strategic choice has costs and benefits. What are you giving up? What are you gaining? What risks are you accepting?

Prioritize Actions: You can't do everything. What's most important? What has to happen first? What can wait? This is Covey's time management matrix applied strategically focus on important-but-not-yet-urgent work.

Build Flexibility: Design strategies that work across multiple scenarios. Avoid commitments that lock you into one path. Create options that let you adjust as situations develop.

The budget contingency strategy I developed with the Governor wasn't about making cuts immediately it was about preparing options we could deploy if needed. We built flexibility to respond to various revenue scenarios without betting everything on one outcome.

Strategic questions to ask:

- What actions could we take now that would position us well regardless of which scenario unfolds?
- What's the earliest we could act while stakes are still low?
- What capabilities or relationships do we need to build now for future opportunities?

- What commitments should we avoid that would limit our future flexibility?
- If we do nothing, what's the likely outcome? Is that acceptable?

PHASE 4: STAGE - POSITION FOR ACTION

The final phase is staging taking early actions that position you to execute your strategy when the time comes. This is the difference between planning and preparing.

Planning means having a strategy on paper. Preparing means putting pieces in place so you can execute quickly when needed. Staging is about creating optionality and reducing friction for future action.

Staging actions include:

Build Capabilities: Develop skills, acquire resources, or create infrastructure you'll need. Do this before you need it urgently.

Example: We developed contingency budget plans before the revenue shortfall materialized, so we had ready options rather than starting from scratch under pressure.

Cultivate Relationships: Build partnerships and alliances you might need. When crisis hits, it's too late to start relationship-building.

Example: We had early conversations with agency heads and legislative leaders about potential scenarios, building shared understanding before decisions were required.

Create Options: Develop multiple pathways so you're not locked into one approach. Options give you flexibility as situations evolve.

Communicate Preparation: Help stakeholders understand what you're seeing and why you're preparing. This builds buy-in and reduces resistance when action becomes necessary.

Establish Triggers: Define indicators that will prompt action. "If X happens, we'll do Y." This converts anticipation into automated response.

The beauty of staging is that it's often invisible. When challenges materialize, people see smooth response and think you're lucky or talented. They don't see the months of preparation that made that response possible. That's fine effective anticipation often looks effortless precisely because it is preparation, not reaction.

Staging principles:

- Act early when stakes are low rather than waiting until pressure is high
- Do preparatory work quietly no need to create alarm before necessary
- Build capabilities that serve multiple scenarios, not just one
- Create "reversible" positioning actions you can adjust if the situation develops differently
- Maintain the discipline to execute staged preparations even when immediate pressure is low

Five Common Strategic Thinking Failures

Over decades of leadership, I've seen leaders consistently make five strategic thinking errors. Understanding these helps you avoid them.

FAILURE 1: CONFUSING ACTIVITY WITH STRATEGY

Many leaders stay busy without being strategic. They're constantly in motion meetings, decisions, initiatives but that motion isn't directional. They haven't defined where they're going, so all the activity is just churning.

Strategy requires pausing to think. It requires creating space to scan, synthesize, and strategize. Leaders who are always in execution mode never develop strategic perspective because they never step back to see the bigger picture.

Fix: Block dedicated time for strategic thinking 2-4 hours weekly where you're not handling operations but thinking about direction, trends, and positioning.

FAILURE 2: EXTRAPOLATING THE PAST INTO THE FUTURE

"We've always done it this way" is the enemy of strategic thinking. Past success doesn't guarantee future results, especially when conditions are changing. Leaders fall into this trap by assuming tomorrow will look like today.

During the 2008 crisis, businesses that assumed conditions would quickly return to pre-crisis patterns struggled. Those that recognized fundamental shifts had changed the landscape adapted better.

Fix: Actively ask "What's different now?" Challenge assumptions about continuity. Look for discontinuities and disruptions, not just trends.

Failure 3: Waiting for Perfect Information

Some leaders avoid strategic positioning because "we don't know enough yet." They wait for certainty before acting. But by the time certainty arrives, early-mover advantages are gone and options are limited. Strategic thinking operates in ambiguity. You'll never have complete information. The question isn't "Are we certain?" but "Do we understand enough to position ourselves intelligently?"

Fix: Act on pattern recognition, not perfect data. Take staged, reversible actions that position you well while maintaining flexibility to adjust as more information arrives.

Failure 4: Ignoring Weak Signals

The most important strategic information often appears as weak signals small indicators that don't seem significant individually. Leaders miss these because they're focused on strong, obvious signals that everyone else also sees. The revenue warning signs I noticed were weak signals. No single indicator screamed "crisis." But together, they formed a pattern that warranted attention.

Fix: Cultivate sensitivity to weak signals. Ask "What are people not talking about yet?" "What small changes might indicate larger shifts?" Pay attention to anomalies and outliers.

Failure 5: Neglecting Implementation Preparation

Some leaders are great at strategy development but terrible

at staging. They create brilliant plans that sit on shelves because they didn't prepare the organization to execute them.

Strategy without staging is just wishful thinking. If you haven't built capabilities, cultivated relationships, and created readiness, your strategy will fail not because it was wrong but because you couldn't execute it.

Fix: For every strategic direction, ask "What needs to be true for us to execute this successfully?" Then systematically build those prerequisites.

AI Applications: Enhancing Strategic Thinking

AI can significantly amplify your strategic thinking capabilities by helping you scan more comprehensively, synthesize patterns faster, explore scenarios more thoroughly, and track implementation more systematically.

Here are five AI applications for strategic anticipation:

AI TOOL 1: TREND ANALYSIS AND PATTERN RECOGNITION

Use AI to scan diverse sources and identify emerging patterns you might miss.

Sample AI Prompt:

"I'm tracking these areas for my organization: [industry sector], [geographic market], [key technologies], [regulatory environment], [workforce trends]. I've noticed these individual signals: [list 5-10 observations from different sources]. Analyze these for: 1) Emerging patterns that connect these signals, 2) Implications for organizations in my sector, 3) Timeline for when impacts might materialize, 4) Weak signals I should pay attention to, 5) Adjacent domains I should monitor. Identify both opportunities and threats."

This helps you synthesize disparate information into strategic insights faster than manual analysis.

AI Tool 2: Scenario Planning and Implications Mapping

Develop comprehensive scenarios and explore their implications systematically.

Sample AI Prompt:

"Based on current trends in [describe situation], create three detailed scenarios for the next 18-24 months: Best Case (favorable developments), Worst Case (challenging developments), and Most Likely Case (realistic middle ground). For each scenario, map out: 1) Key events and milestones, 2) Direct impacts on our organization, 3) Secondary and tertiary effects, 4) Timeline of impacts, 5) Strategic options available, 6) Capabilities we'd need. Our organization profile: [brief description]. Our strategic priorities: [list priorities]."

This creates robust scenario planning that considers multiple futures and their implications.

AI Tool 3: Strategic Option Generator

Expand your strategic thinking by generating options you might not have considered.

Sample AI Prompt:

"We're facing this strategic challenge: [describe situation]. We've identified these obvious options: [list 2-3 conventional approaches].

Help me identify unconventional strategic options by:

1) Suggesting approaches used in analogous situations in other industries,

2) Identifying partnership or collaboration opportunities,

3) Proposing ways to turn constraints into advantages,

4) Recommending positioning moves that would work across multiple scenarios,

5) Highlighting options that competitors might overlook. For each option, explain the logic, key requirements, and potential risks."

This expands your strategic option set beyond conventional thinking.

AI TOOL 4: ASSUMPTION TESTING AND BLIND SPOT IDENTIFICATION

Challenge your strategic thinking to identify assumptions and potential blind spots.

Sample AI Prompt:

"Here's our strategic assessment: [describe your analysis and conclusions]. Challenge this thinking by:

1) Identifying unstated assumptions underlying our analysis,

2) Proposing alternative interpretations of the same data,

3) Highlighting potential blind spots based on our organizational perspective,

4) Suggesting counter-evidence we should consider,

5) Recommending data sources or perspectives we might be missing. Play devil's advocate helps us strengthen our thinking by testing it rigorously."

This helps you avoid confirmation bias and strengthen your strategic analysis.

AI Tool 5: Implementation Roadmap Builder

Convert strategic direction into staged implementation plans.

Sample AI Prompt:

"We've chosen this strategic direction: [describe strategy]. Create a staged implementation roadmap that includes:

1) Phase 1 (0-3 months): Capability building and relationship cultivation,

2) Phase 2 (3-6 months): Option creation and pilot testing,

3) Phase 3 (6-12 months): Scaled implementation with flexibility points,

4) For each phase: specific actions, decision triggers, resource requirements, success metrics,

5) Identify dependencies and sequencing. Build in flexibility to adjust based on how situations develop."

This ensures strategic thinking converts to actionable preparation, not just planning documents.

Reflection Questions

Use these questions to assess your strategic thinking capabilities.

- What percentage of my time is spent on strategic thinking (scanning, synthesizing, strategizing, staging) versus operational execution? Is that the right ratio for my role?
- When was the last time I correctly anticipated a challenge or opportunity months before it materialized?

What pattern recognition enabled that? How can I do it more systematically?

- What weak signals am I currently seeing that I'm dismissing as unimportant? What if those signals are telling me something significant?
- Do I have a systematic scanning routine, or am I relying on information that happens to come my way? What sources should I add to broaden my perspective?
- Am I confusing activity with strategy? Am I busy without being directional? Where am I spending energy that doesn't align with strategic priorities?
- For my current strategic direction, what staging actions am I taking to prepare for implementation? Or am I just planning without preparing?

Action Steps: Building Strategic Thinking This Week

Strategic thinking is a discipline that improves with practice. Choose at least two action steps to implement immediately.

ACTION STEP 1: ESTABLISH A SCANNING ROUTINE

Block 2 hours weekly for strategic scanning and thinking. Use this time to: read industry publications, review economic indicators, talk to frontline staff, monitor competitor moves, and track adjacent domains.

Create a scanning template that guides your attention across different categories. After each session, note 3-5 patterns or signals worth tracking.

ACTION STEP 2: BUILD MULTIPLE SCENARIOS

Identify the most significant uncertainty facing your organization in the next 12-18 months. Develop three scenarios (best case, worst case, most likely case) and map implications for each. Don't bet on one outcome instead, identify actions that would position you well across all three scenarios. Share these scenarios with your team and use them to guide strategic decisions.

ACTION STEP 3: START A STRATEGIC JOURNAL

Create a journal where you document patterns you're seeing, trends you're tracking, and strategic questions you're pondering. Update it weekly. Review it monthly to see how your thinking is evolving. This practice trains pattern recognition and creates a record of your strategic development over time.

ACTION STEP 4: IDENTIFY AND ADDRESS ONE BLIND SPOT

Acknowledge that you have strategic blind spots everyone does. Identify one area where your perspective might be limited (perhaps due to your background, role, or organizational culture). Seek out someone with a different perspective, a peer from another industry, a frontline employee, a customer, a competitor's perspective and ask them what they see that you might be missing.

ACTION STEP 5: STAGE ONE STRATEGIC PREPARATION

Choose one anticipated future scenario and take one staging action this week. Build a capability you'll need, cultivate a relationship that will matter, create an option for future flexibility, or establish a trigger for action. Practice preparing before pressure arrives, not just planning in the abstract.

Chapter Summary: Key Takeaways

- Strategic thinking distinguishes leaders from managers. Managers handle today; leaders prepare for tomorrow through systematic anticipation.
- Anticipation, one of the core leadership principles means seeing what's coming and positioning accordingly. It's about reading patterns, thinking through implications, and acting early when stakes are low.
- The Strategic Anticipation Cycle has four phases: Scan (read signals), Synthesize (connect patterns), Strategize (determine response), Stage (position for action).
- Effective scanning requires widening your aperture beyond immediate domains. Look at industry trends, economic indicators, political/social dynamics, organizational health, and adjacent domains.
- Synthesis converts information into insight by recognizing patterns, mapping implications, projecting timelines, developing scenarios, and challenging assumptions.
- Strategy isn't about predicting one future it's about positioning to succeed across multiple plausible scenarios. Build flexibility and options, not rigid commitments.
- Staging means preparing to execute, not just planning. Build capabilities, cultivate relationships, create options,

communicate preparation, and establish triggers for action.

- Five common failures: confusing activity with strategy, extrapolating the past, waiting for perfect information, ignoring weak signals, and neglecting implementation preparation.
- AI can enhance strategic thinking through trend analysis, scenario planning, option generation, assumption testing, and implementation road mapping.

Stephen Covey teaches us to "Begin with the end in mind." Strategic thinking is about envisioning where you want to end up and positioning yourself to get there anticipating challenges before they arrive, creating options before you need them, and preparing while stakes are still low. The best leaders don't just respond well to crises; they prevent crises through strategic anticipation.

In the next chapter, we'll explore Leading Through Crisis how to apply these strategic capabilities when challenges do materialize and pressure is high. Because even with excellent anticipation, crises still occur. The question is whether you're prepared to lead through them.

The best crises are the ones that never happen because you saw them coming.

Chapter 8

Leading Through Crisis

"It's not over until you win."

Les Brown

37 Hours to Save the Budget

The call came late on a Friday afternoon. I was Director of Budget and Management for the County, and we had a crisis: a critical budget presentation to the legislative leadership was scheduled for Monday at 9 AM. The County Executive needed detailed fiscal analysis and recommendations to navigate a severe revenue shortfall that threatened essential services.

The problem? Our primary computer system, the one containing all the budget models and financial data we needed had crashed. Not just a glitch. A complete system failure. IT estimated recovery would take at least a week, maybe more.

We had 37 hours until that Monday morning presentation. No data. No models. No contingency plan for this scenario. The legislative leaders were expecting comprehensive analysis. The County Executive was depending on us. Failure wasn't an option.

I could see the panic in my team's eyes. Some were already mentally preparing excuses for why we couldn't deliver. But I'd been through enough crises to know that panic never helps and excuses never solve problems.

I called the team together. "Here's our reality," I said calmly. "The system is down. We have 37 hours. We need to deliver. So let's figure out how we're going to do it."

Not 'if we can do it.' Not 'this is impossible.' Just: *How are we going to do it?*

My confidence wasn't fake optimism it was rooted in preparation and trust. I knew my team's capabilities. I knew we had backup data sources, even if they weren't as convenient. I knew we'd built relationships with other agencies that might help. And I knew that in a crisis, people rise to the level of leadership they're given.

We divided into teams. One group manually reconstructed critical data from backup sources and agency records. Another developed simplified models using whatever tools we could access. A third coordinated with other state offices to fill gaps. I stayed in constant communication, removing barriers, making quick decisions, and maintaining calm, confident energy.

People worked through the night. Not because I ordered them to, but because they believed we could succeed. My role wasn't to do the technical work they were better at that than me.

My role was to maintain clarity about what we were accomplishing, confidence that we could accomplish it, and decisive action to remove anything standing in our way.

Sunday evening, we had it. Not perfect, but solid. Comprehensive enough. Defensible. Ready.

Monday morning, the presentation went flawlessly. The legislative leaders got the analysis they needed. The County Executive made informed decisions. The crisis was resolved.

Afterward, team members told me that my confidence made the difference. When the system crashed, they saw disaster. But when I calmly said "Let's figure out how we're going to do this," they shifted from panic to problem-solving. My belief that we could succeed became their belief.

This experience captures the essence of crisis leadership: maintaining composure under pressure, providing clear direction amid chaos, making decisive choices with incomplete information, and inspiring teams to exceed what they thought possible. Crisis doesn't create character it reveals it.

What Crisis Reveals About Leadership

Anyone can lead when conditions are favorable. You know who the real leaders are when things fall apart.

Throughout my career as Chief Administrative Officer, as Chief of Staff to the Governor (the longest-serving in Maryland history), during the 2008 financial crisis with Great Foods LLC, and through countless organizational challenges I've learned that crisis is the ultimate test of leadership capability.

Crisis reveals:

Your True Character: Under pressure, pretense falls away. You can't fake confidence, clarity, or courage when stakes are high. People see who you really are.

Your Preparation: Crisis rewards those who prepared before it arrived. The relationships you built, the capabilities you developed, the scenarios you considered all of that comes into play when pressure hits.

Your Team's Trust: If you've made people feel important, developed their capabilities, and led with integrity (as discussed in previous chapters), they'll follow you through crisis. If you haven't, they won't.

Your Decision-Making: Crisis demands fast decisions with incomplete information. Your judgment, honed through experience and strategic thinking, either serves you well or fails you.

Your Resilience: T.D. Jakes teaches that resilience, the ability to recover from setbacks, is essential for leadership. Crisis tests whether you have the mental toughness to keep going when everything seems to be falling apart.

Les Brown's principle applies powerfully in crisis: "It's not over until you win." Crisis leadership means refusing to accept defeat, continuing to move forward, adapting and adjusting until you find a path to success.

The 2008 financial crisis with Great Foods LLC tested all of these dimensions. Revenue plummeted. The business model we'd built suddenly didn't work. Competitors were closing. Conventional wisdom said we couldn't survive.

But we did survive for another 16 years because we applied crisis leadership principles: stay calm, assess reality honestly, make decisive adjustments, maintain team confidence, and keep moving forward until you win. Crisis didn't end our business; it forced us to become stronger.

Framework: The Crisis Leadership Model

Leading through crisis isn't random, it follows a systematic approach. Based on decades of navigating high-stakes situations, I've developed what I call the Crisis Leadership Model. It has five essential phases that work regardless of the type of crisis you're facing.

The five phases are:

STABILIZE → ASSESS → DECIDE → EXECUTE → LEARN

PHASE 1: STABILIZE - RESTORE ORDER FROM CHAOS

The first moments of a crisis are characterized by chaos, confusion, and often panic. Your immediate priority isn't to solve the crisis, it's to create enough stability that you *can* solve it.

Stabilization has three components:

1. Project Calm Confidence: Your emotional state sets the tone. If you panic, your team panics. If you're calm and confident, they mirror that. This isn't fake optimism it's grounded confidence that you will find a way through.

Example: When the budget system crashed, my first words weren't "This is terrible" but "Let's figure out how we're going to do this." That framing shifted the team from panic to problem-solving immediately.

Your confidence comes from the Confidence Cycle we discussed in Chapter 1 preparation before the moment creates competence that enables confidence during the moment. If you've prepared well (Chapter 7), you have reason for confidence even when things look dire.

2. Stop the Bleeding: Identify what's actively getting worse and take immediate action to prevent further deterioration. You can't solve everything instantly, but you can prevent the situation from spiraling.

Example: During the 2008 crisis at Great Foods LLC, we immediately froze non-essential spending and renegotiated payment terms to preserve cash flow. We couldn't solve the revenue problem instantly, but we could prevent a cash crisis from making things worse.

3. Establish Command Structure: Clarify who's making decisions, who's responsible for what, and how information will flow. Crisis thrives on confusion; clarity kills it.

Example: With the budget crisis, I immediately assigned clear roles: who was reconstructing data, who was building models, who was coordinating with agencies. Everyone knew their responsibility and who had decision authority.

Keys to effective stabilization:

- Control your own emotional response first you can't calm others if you're not calm yourself
- Communicate quickly and clearly what you know, what you don't know, and what you're doing about it

- Take visible action immediately even small steps show leadership and momentum
- Focus on what you can control, not what you can't
- Move quickly but don't rush stabilization requires urgency with deliberateness

PHASE 2: ASSESS - UNDERSTAND THE TRUE SITUATION

Once you've stabilized the immediate situation, you need accurate assessment. This is where many leaders fail they either skip assessment and jump to solutions, or they get paralyzed by analysis.

Effective assessment in crisis requires:

Rapid Information Gathering: Get facts quickly from multiple sources. What actually happened? What's the current state? Who's affected? What resources are available?

In the budget system crisis, I immediately gathered information: What caused the crash? How long for recovery? What backup data exists? Who has relevant expertise? What's our deadline? This took 30 minutes, not 30 hours.

Root Cause Analysis: Understand not just symptoms but underlying causes. Treating symptoms wastes time; addressing root causes solves problems.

Impact Mapping: Who's affected and how? What are first-order, second-order, and third-order effects? This prevents tunnel vision where you solve one problem while creating three others.

Resource Inventory: What capabilities, people, relationships, and assets can you deploy? In crisis, you often have more resources than you initially think you just need to identify them.

Constraint Identification: What are your true constraints? Time? Money? People? Expertise? Knowing constraints helps you focus on viable solutions rather than impossible ones.

Stephen Covey's Habit 5 Seek first to understand, then to be understood is critical here. Don't assume you understand the situation. Ask questions. Listen. Gather perspectives. Your assessment quality determines your solution quality.

Assessment guidelines:

- Set a time box spend enough time to understand, not so much that you delay action
- Talk to people close to the problem they often see things leadership doesn't
- Distinguish facts from assumptions mark clearly what you know vs. what you're inferring
- Look for hidden assets capabilities you already have that could be repurposed
- Update your assessment as new information arrives don't lock into initial understanding

Phase 3: Decide - Make the Call with Incomplete Information

Crisis doesn't wait for perfect information. You must decide with what you have, when you have it. This is where leaders separate from managers the willingness to make consequential decisions under uncertainty.

Decision-making in crisis involves:

Define Success: What does winning look like? Be specific. "Deliver the budget presentation Monday morning with credible analysis" is clearer than "fix the problem."

Generate Options: Quickly develop 3-5 possible approaches. Don't get stuck on one solution. In crisis, you need options because your first idea might not work.

Example: For the budget crisis, options included: postpone the presentation (politically unacceptable), simplify the analysis (possible), manually reconstruct data (labor intensive but doable), or combine simplified approach with targeted reconstruction (best option).

Assess Trade-offs: Every option has costs and benefits. What are you risking? What are you gaining? What's the downside if this doesn't work?

Choose Decisively: Select your path and commit. Indecision in crisis is often worse than an imperfect decision. You can adjust later, but you can't lead while wavering.

Communicate Clearly: Once you've decided, communicate the decision, the rationale, and what you need from people. Use the CLEAR Communication Model from Chapter 3 provide context, ensures understanding, and align on execution.

During my six years as Chief of Staff double the national average tenure, I made countless crisis decisions. The pattern that emerged: decisive action with clear communication creates confidence even when the decision is difficult. Hesitation creates anxiety even when the eventual decision is good.

Decision principles:

- Decide at the right level some decisions you must make,

others should be delegated

- Bias toward action over perfect analysis 80% information is often enough
- Choose reversible decisions when possible maintain flexibility to adjust
- Trust your judgment you have more expertise than you give yourself credit for
- Accept that some decisions will be wrong that's inevitable in crisis, not a failure

PHASE 4: EXECUTE - DRIVE RAPID IMPLEMENTATION

Decisions don't matter if they're not executed. In crisis, execution speed and quality both matter you can't sacrifice one for the other.

Effective crisis execution requires:

Clear Assignments: Everyone knows what they're responsible for, what success looks like, and when it's due. No ambiguity about who does what.

Remove Barriers: Your job as leader is to clear obstacles. People will encounter blockers approval processes, resource constraints, coordination challenges. You intervene quickly to remove them.

Example: During the budget crisis, when a team needed access to agency data that normally required formal requests, I made calls directly to agency heads. When they needed additional staff, I reassigned people immediately. Barrier removal was my primary focus.

Maintain Momentum: In crisis, stopping is dangerous. Keep people moving forward, celebrate small wins, track progress visibly.

Communicate Constantly: Updates every few hours, not every few days. People need to know what's happening, what's changed, what's next. Silence creates anxiety.

Adjust Rapidly: When something isn't working, change course immediately. Crisis execution isn't rigid it's adaptive. Channel the adaptability principles from Chapter 4.

This is where the development work from Chapter 6 pays off. If you've invested in building capable people, they execute with minimal supervision. If you've empowered them (Chapter 5), they make good decisions independently. If you've built trust, they give discretionary effort.

During the budget crisis, team members worked through the night not because I demanded it, but because they believed in our ability to succeed and they trusted my leadership. That trust was built over months and years before the crisis it couldn't be manufactured in the moment.

Execution imperatives:

- Visible leadership be present, be engaged, be available
- Focus on critical path what absolutely must happen for success?
- Empower decision-making at all levels don't create bottlenecks
- Celebrate progress acknowledge effort and achievement frequently

- Maintain your own energy you can't sustain others if you're depleted

PHASE 5: LEARN - EXTRACT LESSONS FOR FUTURE STRENGTH

Most leaders skip this phase. The crisis ends, everyone's exhausted, and they move on without extracting lessons. This is a massive, missed opportunity.

Every crisis contains valuable learning about your systems, your people, your decision-making, your resilience. Leaders who systematically learn from crisis become stronger. Those who don't repeat the same mistakes.

Post-crisis learning involves:

Structured Debrief: Gather key people and systematically review what happened, what worked, what didn't, and why. This isn't about blame it's about understanding.

After the budget crisis, we held a team debrief asking: What enabled our success? What created unnecessary difficulty? What would we do differently? What capabilities should we build to be better prepared next time?

System Improvement: Identify systemic weaknesses the crisis revealed and fix them. Every crisis exposes gaps backup systems that don't exist, processes that break under pressure, dependencies you didn't realize you had.

Capability Building: What skills or resources did you lack? Build them now while lessons are fresh. This is Covey's Habit 7 Sharpen the Saw applied to crisis preparation.

Recognition and Celebration: Acknowledge people who stepped up. Make sure their contributions are recognized. This builds culture and trust for the next crisis.

Documentation: Capture lessons learned in writing. Memory fades. Six months from now, you won't remember critical details. Document now what you learned and what you're changing.

T.D. Jakes teaches that resilience isn't just about bouncing back, it's about bouncing forward, emerging stronger than before. Learning converts crisis from pure cost to strategic investment in future capability.

Learning practices:

- Schedule the debrief while memory is fresh within a week of crisis resolution
- Create psychological safety for honest feedback no punishment for truth-telling
- Focus on systems and processes, not just individual performance
- Turn learning into action creates specific improvement initiatives, not just insights
- Share lessons broadly help the whole organization learn, not just those directly involved

Five Qualities of Effective Crisis Leaders

Beyond the Crisis Leadership Model, certain personal qualities distinguish leaders who excel under pressure from those who crumble. These can be developed over time:

Quality 1: Emotional Regulation

Crisis triggers strong emotions, fear, anxiety, anger, and frustration. Effective leaders feel these emotions but don't let them drive behavior. They maintain composure not by suppressing emotion but by managing its expression.

This connects to self-awareness from Chapter 2 knowing your triggers and having strategies to manage them. When pressure spikes, self-aware leaders recognize their emotional response and consciously choose their reaction rather than defaulting to panic or anger.

Quality 2: Decisive Judgment

Crisis doesn't allow lengthy deliberation. You must make consequential decisions quickly with incomplete information. This requires trusting your judgment even when you can't be certain you're right.

Decisive judgment improves through experience and reflection. Each crisis decision teaches you something. If you learn from them (Phase 5), your judgment strengthens over time.

Quality 3: Adaptive Flexibility

Plans fail in crisis. The path you think will work often doesn't. Effective crisis leaders adapt rapidly changing approaches when necessary, without losing sight of the goal.

This is the adaptability from Chapter 4 applied under extreme pressure. You're not abandoning strategy; you're adjusting tactics to maintain progress toward your objective.

Quality 4: Inspirational Presence

In crisis, people look to their leader for cues about how to respond. Your presence, how you show up, what energy you bring, what you communicate through body language and tone shapes their response.

Inspirational presence doesn't mean cheerleading or false optimism. It means projecting calm confidence, acknowledging reality honestly, and communicating belief that you'll find a way through together.

QUALITY 5: RELENTLESS PERSISTENCE

Les Brown's principle "It's not over until you win" captures this perfectly. Crisis leaders refuse to accept defeat. They keep trying different approaches, learning from failures, adjusting strategies, and moving forward until they succeed.

This isn't stubbornness, it's strategic persistence. You're flexible about methods but unwavering about achieving the mission. You'll find a way, or you'll make a way.

AI Applications: Enhancing Crisis Response

AI can significantly enhance your crisis leadership by providing rapid analysis, scenario planning, decision support, and communication assistance when time is critical.

Here are five AI applications for crisis leadership:

AI TOOL 1: RAPID SITUATION ASSESSMENT

Use AI to quickly analyze complex situations and identify critical factors.

Sample AI Prompt:

"CRISIS SITUATION: [describe what happened]. Help me rapidly assess by providing:

1) Root cause analysis (what triggered this?),

2) Impact mapping (who's affected, first/second/third order effects),

3) Critical constraints (time, resources, authority),

4) Available assets and capabilities,

5) Immediate stabilization actions needed. Organize this in a format I can brief to my team in 5 minutes."

This accelerates Phase 2 (Assess) when every minute matters.

AI Tool 2: Decision Option Generator

Rapidly develop multiple response options with trade-off analysis.

Sample AI Prompt:

"CRISIS: [situation]. GOAL: [what success looks like]. CONSTRAINTS: [time, resources, other limits]. Generate 5 distinct response options ranging from conservative to aggressive. For each option provide:

1) Approach summary,

2) Required resources and timeline,

3) Probability of success,

4) Risks and downsides,

5) Key dependencies. Rank options by risk-adjusted likelihood of achieving the goal."

This supports Phase 3 (Decide) by expanding your option set beyond obvious solutions.

AI TOOL 3: CRISIS COMMUNICATION DRAFTER

Create clear, appropriate communications for different stakeholders quickly.

Sample AI Prompt:

"CRISIS: [situation]. Draft three communications:

1) To my team (acknowledge challenge, explain our response, assign actions, project confidence),

2) To senior leadership (factual update, impact assessment, our plan, support needed),

3) To affected stakeholders (empathy, transparency about what we know/don't know, timeline for resolution). Keep each under 200 words. Tone: calm, clear, confident."

This ensures consistent, appropriate messaging when you're under extreme time pressure.

AI TOOL 4: EXECUTION PLAN BUILDER

Convert decisions into actionable implementation plans with clear assignments.

Sample AI Prompt:

"We've decided on this crisis response: [describe approach].

Create an execution plan with:

1) Workstreams (3-5 parallel efforts),

2) For each workstream: specific actions, owner, timeline, success criteria, dependencies,

3) Critical path (what must happen in sequence),

4) Decision points (when we assess and potentially adjust),

5) Communication cadence (when/how we update stakeholders). Timeline: [X hours/days]. Team size: [Y people]."

This structures Phase 4 (Execute) for rapid, coordinated action.

AI Tool 5: Post-Crisis Debrief Facilitator

Structure comprehensive learning from crisis experience.

Sample AI Prompt:

"We just resolved a crisis: [brief description of what happened and how we responded]. Create a debrief framework covering:

1) Timeline review (key events and decisions),

2) What worked well (capabilities and approaches to preserve),

3) What created difficulty (gaps and weaknesses exposed),

4) Decision quality (which choices were sound, which weren't, and why),

5) System improvements needed,

6) Capability building priorities, 7) Documentation for future reference. Format as discussion guide for team debrief meeting."

This ensures Phase 5 (Learn) produces actionable insights and improvements.

Reflection Questions

Use these questions to assess your crisis leadership capabilities.

- Think about the last crisis I faced. Did I stabilize the situation before trying to solve it, or did I jump straight to solutions while chaos continued?

- How do I typically respond under extreme pressure calm confidence, visible anxiety, or something else? What do my team members see in me during crisis?
- Am I willing to make decisions with incomplete information, or do I wait for certainty that never comes? What's my track record of decisive action in crisis?
- After crises end, do I systematically extract lessons and implement improvements, or do I just move on with relief that it's over?
- Which of the five crisis leader qualities (emotional regulation, decisive judgment, adaptive flexibility, inspirational presence, relentless persistence) is my strength? Which needs development?
- Have I built the relationships, capabilities, and trust before crisis that enable my team to execute effectively during crisis? Or am I trying to create these in the moment?

Action Steps: Preparing for Crisis Leadership

Crisis leadership improves through preparation and practice. Choose at least two action steps to implement immediately.

ACTION STEP 1: PRACTICE EMOTIONAL REGULATION

Identify a current high-pressure situation (doesn't have to be full crisis). Before responding, practice a 10-second pause to regulate your emotional state. Ask yourself: "What emotion am I feeling? What response do I want to have?"

Then choose your reaction consciously rather than defaulting to stress-driven behavior. Practice this regularly to build the muscle for crisis situations.

Action Step 2: Run a Crisis Simulation

Identify a plausible crisis scenario for your organization (system failure, key person departure, major customer loss, etc.). Walk through the Crisis Leadership Model: How would you stabilize? What would you need to assess? What options would you have? How would you execute? Don't wait for real crisis to practice simulate it now while stakes are low.

Action Step 3: Build Crisis Capabilities Now

Identify three capabilities or resources you'd need in a crisis (backup systems, key relationships, emergency procedures, cross-trained staff, etc.). Start building them this week. Don't wait until crisis forces you to develop them under pressure. Prepare when you have time, not when you don't.

Action Step 4: Debrief a Past Crisis

Think about a crisis you handled in the past year. Even if it's over, conduct a structured debrief using Phase 5 (Learn) principles. What worked? What didn't? What capabilities were you missing? What would you do differently? Document the lessons and create specific improvement initiatives based on them.

Action Step 5: Strengthen Your Crisis Team

Crisis leadership depends on team capability. Invest in your team now through the development approaches from Chapter 6. Build their skills, empower their decision-making, create trust and psychological safety. The team you develop in normal times is the team that will execute in crisis times.

Chapter Summary: Key Takeaways

- Crisis reveals true leadership character. Anyone can lead when conditions are favorable; real leaders emerge when things fall apart.
- The Crisis Leadership Model has five phases: Stabilize (restore order), Assess (understand situation), Decide (make the call), Execute (drive implementation), Learn (extract lessons).
- Stabilization creates the foundation for everything else. Project calm confidence, stop the bleeding, and establish clear command structure before trying to solve the crisis.
- Assessment must be rapid but thorough. Gather facts, understand root causes, map impacts, inventory resources, and identify constraints then time-box the analysis and move to decision.
- Decisive action matters more than perfect decisions. Generate options, assess trade-offs, choose your path, and communicate clearly. Indecision is often worse than imperfect decisions.
- Execution requires clear assignments, barrier removal, momentum maintenance, constant communication, and rapid adjustment. This is where preparation and team development pay off.

- Learning converts crisis from pure cost to strategic investment. Debrief systematically, improve systems, build capabilities, recognize contributors, and document lessons.
- Five qualities of crisis leaders: emotional regulation, decisive judgment, adaptive flexibility, inspirational presence, and relentless persistence. These can be developed over time.
- AI can enhance crisis response through rapid situation assessment, option generation, communication drafting, execution planning, and post-crisis learning facilitation.

Les Brown teaches, "It's not over until you win." Crisis leadership is about refusing to accept defeat, continuing to adapt, adjust, and advance until you find a path to success. The question isn't whether you'll face crisis; it's whether you'll be prepared to lead through it.

You've now completed Part II: Leading Others Building High-Performance Teams. You've learned to transition from boss to leader, develop and mentor others, think strategically and anticipate needs, and lead through crisis. These capabilities enable you to build and sustain exceptional teams.

In Part III, we shift focus to Leading Organizations Building Sustainable Excellence on a scale. Chapter 9 begins with creating high-performance culture that persists beyond any individual leader.

Crisis doesn't create character, it reveals it. Prepare now for the crisis you'll face later.

Part III

Leading Organizations - Building Sustainable Excellence

- *Chapter 9: Building Sustainable High-Performance Culture*
- *Chapter 10: AI as Your Leadership Force Multiplier*
- *Chapter 11: Practical AI Tools for Every Leadership Challenge*
- *Chapter 12: Leading the AI-Enabled Organization*

CHAPTER 9

BUILDING SUSTAINABLE HIGH-PERFORMANCE CULTURE

"Culture eats strategy for breakfast."

Peter Drucker

The Culture That Outlasted the Leader

Five years after I left my role as Chief of Staff to Governor Glendening, the longest-serving Chief of Staff in Maryland history I ran into a former colleague who had stayed in state government. Over coffee, she shared something that struck me powerfully.

"The way we work now," she said, "still reflects how you taught us to work. New people join the team and within weeks they start adopting the same standards excellence, anticipation, and service, making people feel important. Nobody explicitly teaches them. They just absorb it because that's the culture we built together."

I was moved by this, but also curious. "What specifically do you see?" I asked.

She smiled. "People still anticipate needs before they become urgent. They still make newcomers feel valued and important from day one. They still hold themselves to higher standards than required. When someone makes a mistake, the focus is on learning, not blame. When someone succeeds, it's celebrated publicly. The phrases you used 'How can we make this excellent?' 'What are we not seeing?' 'Who needs to be developed?' people still say those things."

"But you've been gone five years," I said. "Why hasn't it faded?"

"Because it wasn't about you," she replied. "It was never 'Major's way of doing things.' It was 'our way of doing things.' You made us co-creators of the culture, not just followers of your rules. We owned it. So when you left, we kept it because it was *ours*."

This conversation crystallized something I'd learned over 40+ years of leadership: Sustainable high performance isn't created by brilliant strategies or charismatic leaders it's created by culture. And culture persists only when people own it, not when they merely comply with it.

I saw this pattern again at Great Foods LLC. We operated airport concessions for 20 years surviving the 2008 financial crisis and thriving in a brutally competitive industry. Our competitive advantage wasn't location or pricing. It was culture.

Employees at every level took ownership of excellence, anticipated customer needs, and maintained standards even when nobody was watching. That culture sustained performance year after year, leadership transition after leadership transition.

The question isn't whether culture matters everyone knows it does. The question is: *How do you build culture that sustains high performance beyond any individual leader?*

Why Culture Trumps Strategy

Peter Drucker famously said, "Culture eats strategy for breakfast." After decades of leadership, I've seen this proven repeatedly.

You can have brilliant strategy, but if your culture doesn't support execution, the strategy fails. You can have mediocre strategy, but if your culture is strong people solving problems proactively, maintaining standards autonomously, developing each other continuously you'll outperform organizations with better strategies but weaker cultures.

Here's why culture is more powerful than strategy:

Strategy Changes, Culture Persists: Strategies must adapt to changing conditions. But a strong culture provides stable foundation during change. It's the constant that enables effective adaptation.

Strategy Comes from the Top, Culture Lives Throughout: Leaders develop strategy, but culture is enacted daily by every person in the organization. Culture is what happens when leaders aren't watching.

Strategy Requires Compliance, Culture Creates Commitment: You can mandate strategic initiatives, but you can't mandate cultural ownership. Culture-driven organizations get discretionary effort; strategy-driven organizations get minimum compliance.

Strategy Solves Known Problems, Culture Addresses Unknown Ones: Strategy prepares for anticipated challenges. But culture especially cultures built on principles like anticipation, excellence, and development prepares people to handle whatever emerges.

Leaders Depart, Culture Remains: Your tenure is temporary. If performance depends on your personal presence, it's fragile. Culture that transcends individual leaders is sustainable.

This doesn't mean strategy is unimportant you need both. But culture is the multiplier that determines whether strategy succeeds or fails. Invest in culture first, and strategy execution follows naturally.

Stephen Covey's principle applies here: Private victories precede public victories. Cultural strength (private victory) precedes organizational performance (public victory). Build the culture right, and performance follows.

Framework: The Culture Architecture Model

Building sustainable high-performance culture isn't mystical it's architectural. You design the foundation, construct the structure, and maintain the integrity. I call this the Culture

Architecture Model because culture, like architecture, requires intentional design and continuous maintenance.

The model has four layers:

VALUES (Foundation) → BEHAVIORS (Structure) → SYSTEMS (Reinforcement) → STORIES (Transmission)

Layer 1: Values - The Cultural Foundation

Culture begins with values the core principles that define what matters, what's expected, and what's non-negotiable. But values only matter if they're real, not just words on a wall.

Throughout my career, my core values have been consistent:

- Service - Leadership is about serving others, not being served
- Excellence - Good enough isn't strive for exceptional in everything
- Development - Invest in growing people's capabilities continuously
- Integrity - Do what's right, especially when it's difficult or costly
- Anticipation - Think ahead, prepare proactively, position strategically

These aren't aspirational they're operational. They guide daily decisions. When faced with trade-offs, these values provide the decision criteria.

How to establish authentic values:

Identify What You Actually Value, Not What Sounds Good: Look at how you spend time, what you celebrate, what you won't compromise on. Those reveal your real values. Many organizations claim to value innovation but punish intelligent failures revealing they actually value safety over innovation.

Keep the List Short: Three to five core values maximum. More than that and they're not core they're a laundry list. Core values are the non-negotiables that define your culture.

Define What Each Value Means in Practice: "Excellence" is vague. "Excellence means we proofread every document, we arrive prepared to every meeting, we deliver ahead of deadlines, and we fix problems before they're reported" is specific.

Make Values Co-Created, Not Imposed: When I established culture in new organizations, I engaged people in defining what our values meant and how they'd show up in daily work. This created ownership, not compliance.

Test Values Against Hard Decisions: Values you'll abandon under pressure aren't values they're preferences. Real values guide you especially when they're costly. My integrity value has cost me contracts and opportunities, but never my reputation.

T.D. Jakes emphasizes authenticity in leadership. Authentic values are ones you genuinely live, not ones you market. People see through value statements that leaders don't embody.

Foundation principles:

- Values are demonstrated through leadership behavior first, then taught to others
- When values conflict with short-term results, choose values that's when culture is built or broken
- Hire and promote based on values alignment, not just competence

- Address values violations immediately and publicly (while coaching privately)
- Revisit values periodically to ensure they still reflect what matters most

Layer 2: Behaviors - The Cultural Structure

Values are abstract until translated into specific behaviors. This is where culture becomes visible and tangible. You don't see "excellence" you see people arriving prepared, delivering quality work, and fixing problems proactively.

High-performance cultures have clear behavioral expectations that everyone understands and enacts. These aren't rules imposed from above they're shared standards that people hold each other accountable to maintain.

Key behavioral categories in high-performance cultures:

How We Treat Each Other: In my organizations, making people feel important and valued wasn't optional it was how we operated. New team members were welcomed warmly. Contributions were recognized publicly. People were addressed with respect regardless of role or seniority.

Example: At Great Foods LLC, we made a practice of learning every employee's name within their first week, regardless of position. Managers were expected to know something personal about each team member family, interests, goals. This wasn't manipulation; it was genuine care that created loyalty and discretionary effort.

How We Approach Work: Excellence cultures have specific standards: arrive prepared, meet deadlines early, proofread everything, think through implications before acting, anticipate rather than react.

Example: As Chief of Staff, I established the standard that briefing documents went through three quality checks before reaching the Governor. Not because he demanded it, but because excellence required it. This standard became cultural people maintained it because 'that's how we do things here.'

How We Handle Mistakes: Development cultures treat mistakes as learning opportunities, not occasions for blame. When someone makes an error, the question is "What did we learn?" not "Who's at fault?"

Example: When a team member at Great Foods made a costly ordering error, we used it as a teaching moment for the entire team about verification processes. The person who made the mistake led the training, demonstrating that we value learning and growth over punishment.

How We Communicate: From Chapter 3, we know communication drives performance. In high-performance cultures, people communicate with context, listen to understand, create dialogue, align expectations, and follow through consistently.

How We Develop Others: Development cultures make coaching and mentoring routine, not special. Leaders at every level invest in growing people's capabilities. The phrase "Once you work for Major, you always work for Major" reflects this cultural commitment to development.

How to establish behavioral expectations:

Make Expectations Explicit: Don't assume people know how to behave in your culture. Articulate it clearly. "Here's how we handle disagreements." "Here's our standard for document quality." "Here's how we support each other."

Model Behaviors Consistently: Leaders set the behavioral standard. If you want people to arrive prepared, you arrive prepared. If you want respectful communication, you communicate respectfully. Always. No exceptions.

Reinforce Positive Behaviors Publicly: When someone exemplifies cultural behaviors, acknowledge it publicly. "This is exactly the kind of proactive thinking we value." "This demonstrates our commitment to excellence."

Address Violations Swiftly and Privately: When someone violates cultural standards, address it immediately but privately. Explain why it matters, coach the correct behavior, and ensure accountability.

Create Peer Accountability: The strongest cultures have peer-to-peer accountability, not just top-down enforcement. When people feel ownership of cultural standards, they help each other maintain them.

Behavioral structure principles:

- Behaviors must align with stated values inconsistency destroys credibility
- Leaders get the behaviors they tolerate, not the behaviors they request
- New hires should observe cultural behaviors before they're formally taught 'show then tell'
- High performers who violate cultural values are more damaging than low performers who embody them

- Behavioral standards evolve as organizations grow revisit and refine them periodically

LAYER 3: SYSTEMS - THE CULTURAL REINFORCEMENT

Values and behaviors need systemic reinforcement or they fade under pressure. Systems are the organizational mechanisms that make cultural expectations sustainable.

Key systems that reinforce culture:

Hiring and Onboarding: Hire for cultural fit and technical competence not just one. During onboarding, immerse new people in cultural stories, behavioral expectations, and value demonstrations before throwing them into work.

Example: At Great Foods LLC, new employees spent their first day learning our cultural values and meeting team members before doing any operational work. We paired them with cultural ambassadors high performers who exemplified our standards for their first month.

Performance Management: Evaluate both results and cultural behaviors. Someone who hits targets but violates values shouldn't be rewarded. Someone who embodies values while developing capabilities should be supported.

Example: Our performance reviews explicitly assessed cultural alignment how did you demonstrate service, excellence, development, integrity, and anticipation? Results without values alignment led to coaching plans or separation.

Recognition and Rewards: Celebrate behaviors that exemplify cultural values. Make heroes of people who embody the culture, not just those who deliver results. Recognition shapes what others aspire to.

Example: As Chief of Staff, I created monthly recognition for someone who demonstrated exceptional anticipation, development, or service not just task completion. These recognitions became coveted because they represented cultural ideals.

Development and Training: Invest systematically in developing people's capabilities (Chapter 6). Development cultures don't just talk about growth they resource it with time, budget, and attention.

Decision-Making Processes: Design decision processes that reflect cultural values. If you value integrity, create transparency in decisions. If you value anticipation, build strategic thinking into planning processes. If you value development, involve people in decisions that affect their growth.

Communication Cadences: Regular communication rhythms reinforce culture. Weekly team meetings where you consistently discuss values, celebrate cultural exemplars, and address challenges. Monthly all-hands where you tell cultural stories and reinforce standards.

System design principles:

- Systems should make culturally aligned behavior easier than misaligned behavior
- Audit existing systems for cultural alignment eliminate systems that undermine values

- Consistency matters more than perfection reliable systems build trust
- Resource cultural systems appropriately budget reflects priorities
- Systems should scale design for the organization you're becoming, not just what you are today

LAYER 4: STORIES - THE CULTURAL TRANSMISSION

Culture is transmitted through stories more powerfully than through policies. Stories make values tangible, behaviors memorable, and aspirational standards.

Every organization has stories that people tell and retell about founders, pivotal moments, cultural heroes, values in action. These stories teach new people "how we do things here" more effectively than any manual.

The colleague who told me our cultural practices persisted five years after I left wasn't reciting policies she was telling stories. Stories of anticipation preventing crises. Stories of making newcomers feel valued. Stories of learning from mistakes. These stories carried the culture forward.

Types of stories that transmit culture:

Origin Stories: How the organization or team was founded, what values drove its creation, what principles guided early decisions. These establish cultural DNA.

Value-in-Action Stories: Times when someone upheld values despite cost or difficulty. "Remember when Sarah turned down that lucrative contract because it violated our integrity standards?" These stories make values concrete.

Crisis Response Stories: How the organization handled challenges the 2008 financial crisis, the budget system failure, the leadership transition. These stories reveal what truly matters under pressure.

Cultural Hero Stories: People who exemplified cultural values extraordinarily. Not just leaders, but anyone who demonstrated what excellence, service, or development looks like in practice.

Learning and Growth Stories: Times when mistakes became development opportunities. "Remember when our entire team missed a deadline, and instead of blaming, we rebuilt our project management approach together?" These stories make development cultural.

How to cultivate cultural storytelling:

Tell Stories Regularly: In meetings, in one-on-ones, in communications. Don't just announce decisions, tell the story of why and how. Don't just recognize performance, tell the story of what made it exemplary.

Invite Others to Share Stories: Ask team members to share examples of cultural values in action. "Who saw someone demonstrate excellence this week?" "Tell us about a time when anticipation prevented a problem."

Document and Preserve Stories: Write them down. Record them. Create a cultural story repository. As organizations grow and people turn over, documented stories preserve institutional memory.

Use Stories for Onboarding: New hires should hear the stories that define your culture. Not just facts about the organization stories that reveal what's valued, what's expected, what's celebrated.

Create New Stories Intentionally: When you face decisions, ask: "What story will this create?" Choose actions that create stories you want retold. Cultural legacy is built one story at a time.

Story transmission principles:

- Stories should be authentic, never fabricate or embellish for effect
- The stories people tell reveal what they value listening to identify cultural reality vs. aspiration
- Negative stories spread faster than positive one's address problems before they become cultural legends
- Cultural stories should evolve and create new stories as the organization develops
- Leaders who become part of positive cultural stories create lasting influence

The Leader's Role in Sustaining Culture

While culture must transcend individual leaders to be sustainable, leaders play the critical role in establishing, modeling, and protecting culture. You are the cultural architect, but you're building something that outlasts you.

Five leadership responsibilities for cultural sustainability:

1. Be the Chief Cultural Officer: Culture is your primary responsibility, not an HR function. You set the standard. You

embody the values. You enforce the behaviors. You tell the stories. Culture flows from leadership attention and modeling.

2. Protect Culture During Growth and Change: As organizations grow, culture dilutes unless intentionally maintained. New people, new locations, new pressures all threaten cultural consistency. Your job is vigilant protection of cultural integrity while enabling necessary adaptation.

3. Address Cultural Violations Immediately: Every violation you ignore becomes the new standard. When someone violates values or behavioral expectations, address it swiftly. This isn't about punishment, it's about preservation.

4. Develop Cultural Carriers: Identify and develop people who deeply embody cultural values. These cultural carriers will sustain the culture when you're not present and after you depart. They're your cultural succession plan.

5. Build Culture That Belongs to Everyone: The colleague who said our culture persisted because "it was ours, not yours" captured the essence. Culture you impose doesn't last. Culture people co-create and own does. Make them architects, not just inhabitants.

AI Applications: Building and Sustaining Culture

AI can help you design, assess, and strengthen organizational culture systematically. Here are five applications:

Five AI applications for cultural development:

AI TOOL 1: VALUES CLARITY AND BEHAVIORAL TRANSLATION

Use AI to translate abstract values into concrete behavioral expectations.

Sample AI Prompt:

"Our core organizational values are: [list your 3-5 values]. For each value, help me define: 1) What this value means in practice (specific, observable behaviors), 2) What this value looks like at different organizational levels (executives, managers, frontline staff), 3) How we'd know if someone is embodying this value vs. violating it, 4) Examples of decisions or situations where this value would be tested. Make these concrete enough that anyone could recognize the behaviors."

This creates clarity that prevents values from being meaningless platitudes.

AI TOOL 2: CULTURAL ASSESSMENT AND GAP ANALYSIS

Analyze cultural health and identify gaps between aspiration and reality.

Sample AI Prompt:

"Our stated cultural values are: [list]. Here's what I observe happening in practice: [describe current behaviors, decisions, systems]. Analyze:

1) Where current reality aligns with stated values,

2) Where significant gaps exist between aspiration and practice,

3) What systemic issues might explain the gaps,

4) Which gaps are most critical to address for cultural health,

5) Specific actions to close priority gaps. Be candid about inconsistencies."

This reveals where culture is real vs. aspirational and guides prioritized action.

AI Tool 3: Cultural Story Generator and Curator

Identify and craft stories that transmit cultural values effectively.

Sample AI Prompt:

"Help me develop cultural stories for our value of [value]. Recent events that could become stories: [describe 3-5 situations where this value was demonstrated or tested]. For each, help me:

1) Structure it as a compelling narrative (context, challenge, action, outcome, lesson),

2) Identify what makes it culturally significant,

3) Suggest when and how to share this story (onboarding, team meetings, recognition events),

4) Create questions that help people extract meaning from the story. Keep stories authentic and specific."

This builds a repository of cultural stories that transmit values effectively.

AI Tool 4: Onboarding Cultural Immersion Design

Create comprehensive cultural onboarding that immerses new people in values and behaviors.

Sample AI Prompt:

"Design a 30-day cultural onboarding program for new team members. Our values: [list]. Our key behaviors: [list]. Our cultural stories: [list]. Create:

1) Week-by-week plan for introducing cultural elements,

2) Specific activities that demonstrate each value (not just explain it),

3) People they should meet who exemplify cultural standards,

4) Stories they should hear and why,

5) Reflection questions to assess cultural understanding,

6) How to pair them with cultural ambassadors. Make it experiential, not just informational."

This ensures new hires absorb culture from day one rather than learning it accidentally.

AI Tool 5: Cultural Reinforcement System Audit

Evaluate whether organizational systems reinforce or undermine cultural values.

Sample AI Prompt:

"Our cultural values are: [list]. Here are our current systems: Hiring: [describe process], Performance evaluation: [describe approach], Recognition: [describe what's rewarded], Development: [describe investment], Decision-making: [describe how decisions are made]. Analyze:

1) Which systems strongly reinforce cultural values (and how),

2) Which systems contradict or undermine values (and how),

3) System gaps where we need mechanisms we don't have,

4) Specific modifications to align systems with culture,

5) Priority sequence for system changes. Be specific about the disconnect between stated culture and systemic reality."

This identifies where systems sabotage culture and how to redesign them for alignment.

Reflection Questions

Use these questions to assess your cultural leadership.

- Can I articulate our cultural values in specific, behavioral terms? Or are they vague aspirations that could mean anything?
- Do I consistently model the behaviors I expect from others, or do I exempt myself from cultural standards?
- When have I sacrificed short-term results to protect cultural values? When have I compromised values for results? What pattern does this reveal?
- Do our organizational systems reinforce or contradict our stated values? Where is the biggest misalignment?
- What stories do people tell about our organization? What do those stories reveal about our actual culture vs. our intended culture?
- If I left tomorrow, would our culture persist? Why or why not? Have I built something that belongs to everyone, or something dependent on me?

Action Steps: Building Cultural Foundation This Week

Culture building requires intentional action. Choose at least two action steps to implement immediately.

ACTION STEP 1: DEFINE AND TRANSLATE YOUR VALUES

Identify your 3-5 core cultural values. For each, write specific behavioral definitions what does this value look like in practice? What behaviors demonstrate it? What behavior violates it? Share these with your team and invite their input to refine them. Make values concrete and actionable, not abstract.

ACTION STEP 2: AUDIT ONE SYSTEM FOR CULTURAL ALIGNMENT

Choose one organizational system (hiring, performance management, recognition, decision-making) and evaluate it against your cultural values. Does it reinforce the culture you want or undermine it? Identify one specific change to better align this system with your values and implement it this month.

ACTION STEP 3: TELL A CULTURAL STORY

Identify a recent example where someone exemplified a cultural value perhaps handling a difficult situation with integrity, anticipating a need before it became urgent, or developing a colleague's capabilities. Share this story in your next team meeting, highlighting what made it culturally significant. Start building a practice of cultural storytelling.

ACTION STEP 4: ADDRESS ONE CULTURAL VIOLATION

Identify a behavior you've been tolerating that violates cultural standards. Address it this week privately, constructively, but clearly. Every violation you ignore becomes the new standard. Cultural protection requires swift, consistent action when standards are breached.

ACTION STEP 5: DEVELOP CULTURAL CARRIERS

Identify 3-5 people who deeply embody your cultural values. Invest extra time in developing them not just their technical skills, but their understanding of culture and their capability to transmit it to others. These cultural carriers will sustain the culture when you're not present and after you depart. Make them your cultural succession plan.

Chapter Summary: Key Takeaways

- Culture eats strategy for breakfast. Brilliant strategy fails with weak culture; strong culture enables success even with mediocre strategy. Culture is the multiplier.
- Sustainable culture transcends individual leaders. Culture that depends on one person is fragile; culture that belongs to everyone persists.
- The Culture Architecture Model has four layers: Values (foundation), Behaviors (structure), Systems (reinforcement), Stories (transmission). Each layer is essential.
- Values must be authentic, specific, and consistently demonstrated especially by leaders. Values you'll

abandon under pressure aren't values; they're preferences.

- Behaviors translate values into observable actions. High-performance cultures have clear behavioral expectations that everyone understands and maintains through peer accountability.
- Systems reinforce culture by making aligned behavior easier than misaligned behavior. Audit systems for cultural alignment eliminate those that undermine values.
- Stories transmit culture more powerfully than policies. Cultural stories make values tangible, behaviors memorable, and standards aspirational across generations.
- Leaders are chief cultural officers. You establish values, model behaviors, design systems, tell stories, and protect cultural integrity. This is your primary responsibility.
- AI can enhance cultural development through values translation, gap analysis, story curation, onboarding design, and system auditing.

Peter Drucker teaches us that "culture eats strategy for breakfast." The organizations that outlast their founders, that thrive through leadership transitions, that sustain excellence across decades they all have strong cultures that belong to everyone, not just their current leaders. Your job as a leader isn't to create a culture dependent on you; it's to create a culture that transcends you.

In the next chapter, we'll explore how AI becomes your leadership force multiplier amplifying your capabilities, accelerating your impact, and extending your reach in ways that weren't possible before.

Culture is what remains when the leader leaves. Build something that lasts.

CHAPTER 10

AI AS YOUR LEADERSHIP FORCE MULTIPLIER

"The greatest danger in times of turbulence is not the turbulence it is to act with yesterday's logic."

Peter Drucker

The Consultant Who Tripled His Impact

After spending decades in public service as Chief Administrative Officer, Chief of Staff to the Governor, and running state technology initiatives and then 20 years building Great Foods LLC, I transitioned into consulting through Strategic Solutions Center. The mission was clear: help organizations navigate complex challenges using the leadership principles I'd developed over 40+ years.

But I faced a constraint that every consultant faces: time. I'm one person. I can work with a limited number of clients. I can provide only so many hours of strategic thinking, analysis, and guidance each week. My impact was capped by the hours available to me.

Then I began experimenting with AI as a leadership tool not to replace my expertise, but to amplify it. And the results were transformative.

For a client-facing organizational restructuring, I used AI to rapidly analyze five different structural models, mapping their implications, resource requirements, and implementation pathways. What would have taken me days of manual analysis took hours, allowing me to deliver comprehensive strategic options faster and more thoroughly than ever before.

For another client developing leadership capabilities across their organization, I used AI to create personalized development plans for 30 emerging leaders simultaneously each plan customized to the individual's current capabilities, growth goals, and organizational needs. Previously, I could have created maybe 5-6 truly customized plans in the same timeframe.

For a third client navigating a crisis, I used AI to generate multiple scenario analyses, risk assessments, and response strategies in real-time during our strategy sessions. The speed enabled us to explore far more options and think through implications more thoroughly than traditional analysis allowed.

Within six months of integrating AI systematically into my consulting practice, I'd tripled the number of clients I could serve effectively while *increasing* the depth and quality of work for each. Not because I was working longer hours I wasn't. But because AI became my force multiplier.

Here's what I learned: AI doesn't replace leadership it amplifies it. AI handles the analytical heavy lifting, the pattern recognition, the option generation, the documentation. This frees leaders to do what only humans can do: exercise judgment, build relationships, provide wisdom, make consequential decisions, and inspire commitment.

The leaders who thrive in the AI era won't be those who resist the technology or those who blindly defer to it. They'll be those who learn to partner with AI strategically using it to extend their capabilities, accelerate their impact, and focus their energy on the highest-value leadership activities.

Understanding the AI Leadership Partnership

Peter Drucker warned against acting with yesterday's logic in times of turbulence. We're in such a time. AI represents a fundamental shift in how leadership work gets done comparable to how personal computers, the internet, and mobile technology each transformed work in their eras.

But here's the crucial distinction: AI is not just another productivity tool. It's a *thinking partner* that can extend your cognitive capabilities in ways no previous technology could.

Think about the evolution:

- Calculators automated arithmetic but couldn't think about what to calculate
- Spreadsheets automated data manipulation but couldn't interpret what the data meant

- Databases stored information but couldn't synthesize insights from it
- AI can analyze, synthesize, generate, evaluate, and reason about information cognitive tasks that previously only humans could do

This creates a partnership model where:

AI Handles: Pattern recognition across massive data, rapid option generation, comprehensive analysis, documentation, research synthesis, routine decision support, scenario modeling, initial drafts and frameworks

Leaders Handle: Final judgment calls, relationship building, values-based decisions, strategic direction, cultural stewardship, coaching and development, inspirational communication, ethical considerations

The partnership works because AI and humans have complementary strengths. AI never gets tired, can process volumes of information instantly, has no ego or bias beyond what's in its training, and generates options without being constrained by conventional thinking. Humans bring wisdom from experience, emotional intelligence, ethical judgment, relationship capabilities, and contextual understanding that AI lacks.

The key insight: AI amplifies your existing capabilities. If you're already a strong strategic thinker, AI makes you faster and more comprehensive. If you're skilled at development, AI helps you scale personalized coaching. If you excel at crisis response, AI accelerates your assessment and option generation. It multiplies what you already do well.

Framework: The AI Leadership Multiplier Model

Based on my experience integrating AI into leadership work, I've developed what I call the AI Leadership Multiplier Model. It identifies five key domains where AI multiplies leadership effectiveness.

The five multiplier domains are:

ANALYSIS → GENERATION → PERSONALIZATION → ACCELERATION → DOCUMENTATION

DOMAIN 1: ANALYSIS MULTIPLIER - SEE MORE, SEE FASTER

Leaders spend enormous time analyzing situations reading reports, studying data, identifying patterns, assessing implications. AI can compress weeks of analytical work into hours while often surfacing insights humans might miss.

How AI multiplies analytical capability:

Comprehensive Pattern Recognition: Give AI multiple reports, datasets, or documents and ask it to identify patterns, trends, anomalies, and connections. It processes information faster and more completely than humans reading sequentially.

Example: I provided AI with three years of client performance data, market analysis reports, and competitive intelligence. Asked it to identify emerging patterns and strategic implications. It surfaced five significant trends I hadn't fully connected trends that shaped subsequent strategic recommendations.

Multi-Perspective Analysis: Ask AI to analyze the same situation from the perspectives of different stakeholders' customers, employees, investors, competitors, and regulators. This surfaces blind spots and builds more comprehensive understanding.

Root Cause Identification: Present AI with a problem and ask it to work backwards to potential root causes. It can generate hypotheses you can then test, accelerating diagnostic work.

Implication Mapping: From Chapter 7, we know strategic thinking requires mapping first, second, and third-order implications. AI excels at this, taking a proposed action and systematically exploring cascading effects.

Comparative Analysis: Give AI multiple options (strategic approaches, organizational structures, budget scenarios) and ask for systematic comparison across defined criteria. It produces comprehensive comparison matrices quickly.

This analytical multiplier doesn't replace your judgment, it feeds it. AI does the heavy analytical lifting; you apply wisdom, experience, and contextual understanding to interpret findings and make decisions.

Analysis multiplier practices:

- Always verify AI analysis against your own observations and expertise
- Use AI to challenge your assumptions, ask it to argue against your conclusions
- Provide AI with context about your organization, industry, and constraints for more relevant analysis

- Be specific about what you need vague requests get vague analysis
- Iterate on analysis follow-up questions often yield the deepest insights

DOMAIN 2: GENERATION MULTIPLIER - CREATE MORE OPTIONS

Leaders often get stuck in conventional thinking considering only the obvious options because generating alternatives is mentally taxing. AI is tireless at option generation and unconstrained by conventional wisdom.

How AI multiplies generative capability:

Strategic Option Generation: Describe a challenge and ask AI to generate 10 distinct approaches from conservative to radical. This expands your strategic option set beyond what you'd think of alone.

Example: A client was considering two approaches to organizational restructuring. I asked AI to generate eight additional structural models. Three of those AI-generated options became serious considerations, and one was ultimately selected an option we likely wouldn't have explored without AI prompting.

Communication Drafting: From Chapter 3, we know communication quality matters. AI can draft speeches, emails, presentations, or announcements based on your key messages. You edit and refine but start from a solid draft rather than a blank page.

Framework and Model Creation: Describe a concept and ask AI to create a framework, model, or structure for it. It can generate visual diagrams, process flows, decision trees, or analytical frameworks quickly.

Question and Prompt Development: Need powerful coaching questions? Effective meeting agendas? Strategic thinking prompts? AI generates these rapidly, drawing from vast patterns of effective questioning.

Scenario Development: For strategic planning (Chapter 7), AI can generate detailed scenarios best case, worst case, most likely, and alternative futures you hadn't considered. This strengthens anticipation and preparedness.

The generation multiplier doesn't replace your creativity it augments it. AI generates raw material; you select, refine, and apply judgment about what's actually viable and appropriate.

Generation multiplier practices:

- Generate quantity first, evaluate quality second get 10 options, then choose best 2-3
- Specify constraints and criteria to guide generation toward useful options
- Use AI-generated content as starting points, not finished products
- Ask AI to explain its reasoning behind generated options to understand the logic
- Combine AI-generated options with your own ideas for hybrid approaches

Domain 3: Personalization Multiplier - Scale Individual Attention

One of the hardest leadership constraints is personalizing

attention treating each person as an individual with unique needs, capabilities, and circumstances. AI enables personalization at scale previously impossible.

How AI multiplies personalization capability:

Individual Development Plans: From Chapter 6, we know development matters. Provide AI with information about someone's current capabilities, goals, and context. It can generate personalized development plans customized to that individual.

Example: I created 30 personalized leadership development plans using AI each tailored to the individual's strengths, gaps, learning style, and organizational role. What would have taken weeks of one-on-one work was completed in days, and the quality was excellent because I could focus energy on customization rather than basic structure.

Customized Coaching: Describe someone's specific situation and ask AI for coaching questions, feedback frameworks, or development approaches tailored to their needs. This strengthens your one-on-one coaching effectiveness.

Adaptive Communication: Draft messages to different stakeholders on the same topic, customized to each audience's interests, concerns, and communication preferences. AI handles the customization work.

Individual Recognition: Making people feel important (core principle) requires specific recognition. AI can help draft personalized recognition messages that highlight individual contributions meaningfully rather than generic praise.

Tailored Learning Resources: Ask AI to curate learning resources (articles, books, exercises, frameworks) matched to someone's specific development needs, learning preferences, and time constraints.

The personalization multiplier enables the development focus I've always valued but couldn't fully scale. AI handles customization logistics; I provide the human connection, judgment about what's truly needed, and relationship investment that makes development stick.

Personalization multiplier practices:

- Provide AI with detailed context about individuals to enable genuine customization
- Review and refine AI-generated personalized content add personal touches only you know
- Use AI for structure and scale, but deliver personally don't let it feel automated
- Combine AI-enabled personalization with genuine human connection and care
- Protect privacy be thoughtful about what personal information you provide to AI

Domain 4: Acceleration Multiplier - Move Faster Without Sacrificing Quality

Speed matters in leadership. Delayed decisions, slow communication, sluggish analysis all create competitive disadvantage. But speed usually trades off against quality. AI breaks that trade-off.

How AI multiplies speed capability:

Rapid Research and Synthesis: Need to understand a new topic, industry, or trend quickly? AI can synthesize information from multiple sources in minutes, creating comprehensive briefings that would take hours of reading.

Example: A client needed to make a decision about entering a new market segment. I used AI to synthesize market research, competitive analysis, regulatory considerations, and financial modeling in 90 minutes. We had strategic options ready for discussion that afternoon rather than waiting days for traditional analysis.

Real-Time Decision Support: In meetings or crisis situations (Chapter 8), use AI to generate options, analyze trade-offs, or model scenarios in real-time. This accelerates decision-making without sacrificing thoroughness.

Quick Iteration: Draft a strategy, plan, or communication and ask AI for critique and improvement suggestions. Iterate multiple times rapidly to reach high quality faster than traditional revision cycles.

Accelerated Learning: Need to get up to speed on a new domain? AI can create customized learning paths, summarize key concepts, generate practice scenarios, and answer questions compressing learning time significantly.

Fast Follow-Through: After meetings, use AI to draft follow-up communications, action item tracking, or decision documentation quickly. This ensures momentum doesn't lag due to administrative work.

The acceleration multiplier is particularly valuable for strategic thinking (Chapter 7) and crisis response (Chapter 8) where time pressure is intense. AI handles time-consuming analytical and generative work so you can focus cognitive energy on judgment and decision-making.

Acceleration multiplier practices:

- Fast doesn't mean careless always review AI output before acting on it
- Use acceleration for time-sensitive work, not as default for everything
- Build AI prompts and workflows in advance for situations requiring rapid response
- Balance speed with reflection some decisions benefit from deliberation
- Document AI-accelerated processes so you can replicate them efficiently

Domain 5: Documentation Multiplier - Capture Knowledge Systematically

Leaders often fail to document decisions, lessons learned, or institutional knowledge because documentation feels like administrative burden. This creates organizational amnesia. AI makes documentation effortless.

How AI multiplies documentation capability:

Meeting Documentation: Provide AI with meeting notes or recordings and ask it to create structured documentation decisions made, action items, key discussions, follow-up needed. This preserves institutional knowledge automatically.

Process Documentation: Describe how something works and ask AI to create formal process documentation steps, responsibilities, decision points, exceptions. This builds organizational capability independent of individual knowledge.

Lessons Learned Capture: From Chapter 8, we know crisis

learning matters. After any significant event, use AI to structure lessons learned documentation what happened, what worked, what didn't, what to change, what to preserve.

Decision Documentation: Record the logic behind important decisions options considered, criteria used, trade-offs assessed, rationale selected. AI can structure this so future leaders understand "why we decided what we decided."

Knowledge Transfer: Capture expert knowledge from experienced people before they leave. AI can interview (via prompts), structure, and document their expertise for organizational preservation.

The documentation multiplier prevents organizational memory loss. From my experience across county government, state leadership, and Great Foods LLC, I've seen how much knowledge walks out the door when people leave. AI makes knowledge capture systematic rather than sporadic.

Documentation multiplier practices:

- Create documentation templates AI can populate maintains consistency
- Document while events are fresh AI can't capture what's forgotten
- Make documentation searchable and accessible captured knowledge must be findable
- Review AI-generated documentation for accuracy before finalizing
- Build documentation culture make it expected, not exceptional

Getting Started: Your AI Integration Roadmap

The AI Leadership Multiplier Model shows *what's* possible. But *how* do you actually integrate AI into your leadership practice? Here's the roadmap I followed and recommend to clients:

Phase 1: Experiment and Learn (Weeks 1-4)

Start by experimenting with AI for low-stakes tasks. Don't bet your most important work on AI until you understand its capabilities and limitations.

- Choose one multiplier domain to focus on initially (I started with Analysis)
- Identify 3-5 routine tasks where AI might help and test it on those
- Compare AI output to your own work to calibrate quality expectations
- Document what works and what doesn't build your own AI usage patterns

Phase 2: Build Core Workflows (Weeks 5-12)

Once you've learned AI capabilities, build systematic workflows for recurring leadership tasks.

- Create template prompts for tasks you do repeatedly (meeting prep, decision analysis, communication drafting)
- Develop personal AI workflows that integrate into your existing work rhythms
- Expand to a second multiplier domain (add Generation

after mastering Analysis)

- Track time saved and quality improvement to validate the investment

PHASE 3: SCALE AND OPTIMIZE (MONTHS 4-6)

Once core workflows are working, scale AI usage across more domains and optimize efficiency.

- Integrate all five multiplier domains into regular practice
- Share effective AI workflows with your team multiply the multiplier effect
- Refine prompts and workflows based on accumulated experience
- Identify strategic opportunities where AI enables entirely new capabilities

PHASE 4: STRATEGIC INTEGRATION (ONGOING)

AI integration becomes strategic advantage when it's woven into organizational capability, not just personal productivity.

- Build organizational AI capabilities team workflows, shared prompts, collective learning
- Use AI to enable capabilities previously impossible (personalized development at scale, comprehensive scenario planning)
- Continuously evolve AI usage as technology advances and your expertise deepens
- Maintain human-centric leadership while leveraging AI amplification

Five Critical Principles for Effective AI Partnership

As you integrate AI into leadership practice, these five principles ensure you harness its power without compromising leadership effectiveness:

Principle 1: AI Amplifies, Never Replaces, Human Judgment

AI provides analysis, options, and recommendations. You provide the judgment especially on values-based decisions, people matters, and strategic direction. Never defer final judgment to AI. It's a tool that informs your decisions, not a substitute for your leadership.

Principle 2: Verify Critical AI Output

AI makes mistakes factual errors, logical inconsistencies, inappropriate recommendations. For consequential work, verify AI output against other sources, your expertise, and common sense. Trust but verify, especially early in your AI journey.

Principle 3: Maintain Human Connection in AI-Augmented Leadership

Use AI for analysis and preparation, but maintain genuine human connection with people. Don't let AI-drafted communications feel automated. Don't let AI-enabled personalization replace authentic care. The principle of making people feel important and valued requires human presence, not just AI efficiency.

PRINCIPLE 4: BE TRANSPARENT ABOUT AI USAGE WHEN APPROPRIATE

You don't need to disclose every AI usage, but when sharing AI-generated analysis or content with teams, be transparent. "I used AI to analyze these options" builds trust. Trying to pass off AI work as entirely your own erodes it. Integrity (core value) requires honesty.

PRINCIPLE 5: CONTINUOUSLY DEVELOP YOUR AI CAPABILITY

AI capabilities are evolving rapidly. What's impossible today may be routine in six months. Maintain a learning posture experiment with new AI capabilities, share discoveries with colleagues, refine your approaches. This is Covey's Habit 7 (Sharpen the Saw) applied to AI partnership.

Reflection Questions

Use these questions to assess your AI integration opportunity.

- What leadership tasks consume significant time but could be partially automated or accelerated through AI? Where is my time going that AI could help reclaim?
- Which of the five multiplier domains (Analysis, Generation, Personalization, Acceleration, Documentation) would create the most immediate value for me? Where should I start?
- What leadership capabilities do I wish I could scale but can't due to time constraints? Could AI enable that scaling?

- Am I approaching AI with appropriate balance neither dismissing it as hype nor treating it as magic? Do I understand both its capabilities and limitations?
- How might AI enable me to spend more time on the highest-value leadership activities coaching, strategic thinking, relationship building by handling lower-value tasks?
- What concerns do I have about AI integration? Are these concerns based on understanding or assumptions? How can I test my concerns through careful experimentation?

Action Steps: Starting Your AI Multiplication Journey

AI integration requires deliberate action. Choose at least two action steps to implement immediately.

Action Step 1: Choose Your Starting Domain

Select one of the five multiplier domains to focus on for the next 30 days. Choose based on where you spend significant time or where you see clear opportunity. Commit to experimenting with AI for that domain at least three times weekly. Document what you learn.

Action Step 2: Create Your First AI Workflow

Identify one recurring leadership task (weekly meeting prep, monthly reporting, decision analysis, communication drafting) and develop an AI workflow for it. Create a template prompt, test it, refine it, and use it consistently for a month. Measure time saved and quality delivered.

ACTION STEP 3: TEST AI FOR A CURRENT CHALLENGE

Take a current leadership challenge you're facing and use AI to help address it. Perhaps generating strategic options, analyzing a complex situation, drafting communications, or developing personalized coaching approaches. Compare AI-assisted work to how you'd tackle it without AI. Assess the value honestly.

ACTION STEP 4: SHARE AI CAPABILITIES WITH YOUR TEAM

Once you've found an AI workflow that works well, share it with your team. Show them the prompt, the output, and how you use it. Encourage them to experiment and share their own discoveries. Build collective AI capability, not just personal productivity.

ACTION STEP 5: SCHEDULE AI LEARNING TIME

Block 2 hours monthly for AI learning and experimentation. Use this time to try new AI capabilities, refine existing workflows, learn from others' AI usage, or explore emerging AI tools. Make continuous AI capability development systematic, not sporadic. This is investment in your future leadership effectiveness.

Chapter Summary: Key Takeaways

- AI is a force multiplier for leadership it amplifies capabilities, accelerates impact, and enables previously impossible scale. Leaders who partner with AI strategically will significantly outperform those who don't.

- AI is a thinking partner, not just a productivity tool. It can analyze, synthesize, generate, and reason cognitive tasks previously requiring human intelligence.
- The AI Leadership Multiplier Model identifies five domains: Analysis (see more, see faster), Generation (create more options), Personalization (scale individual attention), Acceleration (move faster without sacrificing quality), Documentation (capture knowledge systematically).
- AI handles analytical and generative heavy lifting; leaders provide judgment, wisdom, relationship building, and ethical guidance. It's partnership, not replacement.
- Integration follows a roadmap: Experiment and Learn (weeks 1-4), Build Core Workflows (weeks 5-12), Scale and Optimize (months 4-6), Strategic Integration (ongoing).
- Five critical principles: AI amplifies but never replaces human judgment, verify critical output, maintain human connection, be transparent about usage, continuously develop AI capability.
- Start with one domain, create workflows for recurring tasks, share discoveries with your team, and maintain continuous learning posture.

Peter Drucker warns us not to act with yesterday's logic in times of turbulence. AI represents a fundamental shift in leadership capability those who learn to partner with it effectively will multiply their impact exponentially. But AI is a tool, not a substitute. It amplifies your leadership; it doesn't replace it. Your judgment, wisdom, relationships, and values remain uniquely human and irreplaceable.

In Chapter 11, we'll get practical specific AI tools and prompts for every leadership challenge covered in this book. You'll have a comprehensive toolkit for AI-enhanced leadership.

The future belongs to leaders who multiply their impact through intelligent AI partnerships.

CHAPTER 11

PRACTICAL AI TOOLS FOR EVERY LEADERSHIP CHALLENGE

"An ounce of practice is worth more than tons of preaching."

Mahatma Gandhi

You've learned the concepts. You've seen the frameworks. You understand the AI Leadership Multiplier Model. Now it's time to get practical.

This chapter is your AI leadership toolkit specific prompts, workflows, and applications for every major leadership challenge covered in this book. Think of it as your reference guide: when you face a particular leadership situation, come to this chapter, find the relevant tool, and use it.

Each tool follows a consistent structure:

- The leadership challenge it addresses
- The AI prompt to use (which you can customize)

- How to use the output effectively
- Key considerations for best results

These aren't rigid scripts, they're starting points. Adapt them to your context, your style, and your specific needs. The goal is practical application, not theoretical understanding.

Part I: Leading Yourself - AI Tools for Personal Leadership

TOOL 1: CONFIDENCE ASSESSMENT AND DEVELOPMENT PLAN

Leadership Challenge: You want to build authentic confidence through the Confidence Cycle (Preparation → Competence → Confidence → Performance) but need a systematic approach.

AI Prompt:

"I'm working on building authentic confidence in [specific area: public speaking / strategic decision-making / crisis leadership / etc.]. Help me create a development plan using the Confidence Cycle framework (Preparation → Competence → Confidence → Performance). My current situation: [describe where you are now]. My confidence gap: [what you lack confidence in]. Create:

1) Specific preparation actions I can take to build competence,

2) Incremental performance opportunities to test growing competence,

3) Reflection practices to reinforce confidence from successful performance,

4) A 90-day roadmap for confidence building, 5) Success metrics to track progress. Focus on practical, actionable steps."

How to Use the Output:

- Review the preparation actions and select 2-3 to start immediately
- Schedule the incremental performance opportunities on your calendar
- After each performance opportunity, use the reflection practices to extract learning
- Track progress monthly against the success metrics

Key Consideration: Authentic confidence comes from actual competence, not affirmations. Focus your energy on the preparation and competence-building activities, not on trying to "feel" confident.

Tool 2: Leadership Identity Mapping

Leadership Challenge: You need deeper self-awareness about your leadership style, triggers, strengths, and blind spots.

AI Prompt:

"Help me map my leadership identity using the Leadership Identity Matrix. Here's information about me: Natural strengths: [list what you do well naturally]. Learned capabilities: [skills you've developed]. Values I won't compromise: [core principles]. Situations where I excel: [contexts where you're most effective]. Situations where I struggle: [contexts where you're less effective]. Feedback I've received (both positive and developmental): [themes from feedback]. Based on this, create:

1) My leadership identity profile (who I am as a leader),

2) My natural leadership style and when it serves me well,

3) My triggers and stress responses (what activates my worst tendencies),

4) My blind spots (what I might not see about myself),

5) Development areas to address gaps between current identity and leadership requirements."

How to Use the Output:

- Share the leadership identity profile with trusted colleagues to verify accuracy
- Create awareness triggers for your identified stress responses and blind spots
- Build compensating strategies for situations where your natural style doesn't serve you
- Revisit and update the map quarterly as you develop new capabilities

Key Consideration: Self-awareness requires honesty. Provide AI with accurate information, including uncomfortable truths about your weaknesses. The quality of self-awareness depends on the honesty of your input.

TOOL 3: CLEAR COMMUNICATION MESSAGE BUILDER

Leadership Challenge: You need to deliver high-stakes communication (presentation, difficult conversation, organizational announcement) using the CLEAR model (Context, Listen, Engage, Align, Results).

AI Prompt:

"Help me structure high-impact communication using the

CLEAR model. My situation: [describe what you need to communicate and to whom]. My objectives: [what you want to achieve]. Audience considerations: [what they care about, what concerns they might have]. Using the CLEAR framework, create:

1) CONTEXT: Opening that establishes why this matters and what's at stake,

2) LISTEN: Questions I should ask to understand their perspective before presenting mine,

3) ENGAGE: Core message that creates dialogue (not monologue), specific stories or examples that make abstract concepts tangible,

4) ALIGN: Explicit statements of what we're agreeing to and what success looks like,

5) RESULTS: Follow-through actions and accountability mechanisms. Make it conversational, not corporate."

How to Use the Output:

- Customize the context and stories to reflect your authentic voice don't read AI output verbatim
- Actually use the listening questions don't skip to your message
- Practice the communication aloud to ensure it flows naturally
- After the communication, reflect on what worked and what didn't to improve future use

Key Consideration: Communication effectiveness depends on authentic delivery, not perfect words. Use AI for structure, but make the delivery genuinely yours.

TOOL 4: CHANGE ADAPTATION STRATEGY

Leadership Challenge: You're facing significant change and need a systematic approach to adapt effectively using the Adaptability Compass.

AI Prompt:

"I'm navigating significant change: [describe the change organizational restructure, new role, market disruption, technology shift, etc.]. Help me create an adaptation strategy using the Adaptability Compass framework. My situation: [current state]. The change: [what's different]. Implications for me: [how this affects your role/work/team]. Create:

1) Assessment of what must change vs. what should stay the same (don't adapt everything),

2) Core capabilities I need to maintain vs. new capabilities to develop,

3) Potential resistance points (in me or others) and how to address them,

4) Quick wins to build adaptation momentum,

5) 90-day adaptation roadmap with specific milestones,

6) Reflection practices to learn and adjust as I adapt. Focus on practical adaptation, not just acceptance."

How to Use the Output:

- Start with the quick wins to create positive momentum early
- Address resistance points proactively before they become blockers

- Use the reflection practices bi-weekly to assess what's working and adjust strategy
- Share the adaptation roadmap with stakeholders to create shared understanding

Key Consideration: Adaptability is active, not passive. You're making deliberate choices about how to change, not just accepting whatever happens.

Part II: Leading Others - AI Tools for Team Leadership

Tool 5: Boss-to-Leader Transition Plan

Leadership Challenge: You're transitioning from directive management to developmental leadership and need specific behavioral changes.

AI Prompt:

"I'm working on transitioning from boss to leader using the Leadership Transition Matrix (Directing→Developing, Controlling→Empowering, Telling→Asking, Managing Work→Leading People). My current tendencies: [describe how you typically lead now be honest about directive habits]. My team: [brief description of team capabilities and maturity]. Create:

1) Specific behavioral shifts I need to make in each transition area,

2) Situations where I default to 'boss' mode and how to catch myself,

3) Coaching questions I can use instead of directive statements,

4) Empowerment boundaries I can establish (outcomes, constraints, authority, support),

5) Weekly practices to reinforce developmental leadership,

6) Metrics to assess whether people are becoming more capable and autonomous. Be specific about what to stop doing and what to start doing."

How to Use the Output:

- Share your transition goals with your team be transparent that you're working on leading differently
- Use the coaching questions daily make them habitual before situations arise
- After each interaction where you default to directive mode, reflect on what triggered it
- Track team capability and autonomy monthly true leadership shows in their growth

Key Consideration: Transitioning from boss to leader means tolerating initial inefficiency as people learn. Resist the urge to "just do it yourself" when they struggle.

TOOL 6: PERSONALIZED DEVELOPMENT PLAN CREATOR

Leadership Challenge: You want to create customized development plans for team members using the Development Pipeline framework.

AI Prompt:

"Create a personalized development plan for a team member using the Development Pipeline (Identify →Invest →Stretch →Support →Release). Person's profile: Name: [name], Current role: [role], Strengths: [what they do well], Development areas: [capabilities to build], Career aspirations: [where they want to grow], Learning style: [how they learn best], Constraints: [time, budget, other limits]. Using the framework, create:

1) IDENTIFY: Specific high-potential capabilities to develop based on their profile,

2) INVEST: Direct time commitment (monthly 1-on-1s, specific coaching topics), Access/Exposure opportunities (meetings, projects, relationships),

3) STRETCH: 3-5 stretch assignments calibrated to challenge without overwhelming,

4) SUPPORT: Real-time coaching triggers, problem-solving partnership approach, resources needed,

5) RELEASE: Milestones for increased autonomy, success criteria for advancement. Make it a 6-month plan with specific, actionable steps."

How to Use the Output:

- Review the plan with the person make it collaborative, not imposed
- Schedule the investment time on your calendar immediately protected, not optional
- Assign stretch opportunities progressively don't pile them all on at once
- Review progress monthly and adjust plan based on what's working

Key Consideration: Development requires genuine

investment time, attention, advocacy. If you're not willing to invest, don't create the plan.

TOOL 7: STRATEGIC ANTICIPATION SCENARIO BUILDER

Leadership Challenge: You need to think strategically about future scenarios and prepare proactively using the Strategic Anticipation Cycle.

AI Prompt:

"Help me apply strategic anticipation using the Scan →Synthesize →Strategize→Stage framework. My focus area: [market conditions, organizational changes, competitive dynamics, regulatory environment, technology trends, etc.]. Current observations: [list 8-10 signals you're seeing from diverse sources]. Create:

1) SCAN: Additional signals I should be monitoring that I might be missing,

2) SYNTHESIZE: Emerging patterns from the signals (what story do they tell?), Timeline projection (when impacts will likely materialize), Three scenarios: Best Case, Worst Case, Most Likely Case with specific narrative for each,

3) STRATEGIZE: For each scenario, what strategic positioning would serve us well?, Actions that work across all scenarios (robust strategies),

4) STAGE: Immediate preparation actions (next 30 days), Capabilities to build proactively, Relationships to cultivate, Triggers that would prompt full execution. Focus on preparation, not prediction."

How to Use the Output:

- Focus on the staging actions these create optionality regardless of which scenario unfolds
- Share scenarios with leadership team to build shared understanding
- Update scenarios quarterly as new information emerges
- Execute staging actions even when pressure is low that's when preparation is easiest

Key Consideration: Strategic anticipation is about preparation, not prophecy. Build capabilities and options now for challenges you might face later.

Tool 8: Crisis Leadership Action Plan

Leadership Challenge: You're facing a crisis and need rapid, systematic response using the Crisis Leadership Model.

AI Prompt:

"CRISIS SITUATION: [describe what happened]. TIME CONSTRAINT: [when response is needed]. Help me apply the Crisis Leadership Model

(Stabilize→Assess→Decide→Execute→Learn).

Create: 1) STABILIZE: Immediate actions to stop deterioration and restore basic order, Communication to project calm confidence (draft brief message to team), Command structure (who decides what, information flow), 2) ASSESS: Critical information needed for decisions, Root cause analysis (what triggered this), Impact mapping (who's affected, cascading effects), Resource inventory (what we have available), 3) DECIDE: Success definition (what does resolved look like?), 5 response options (from conservative to aggressive), Recommended option with rationale, 4) EXECUTE: 3-5 parallel workstreams with owners, Critical path (must-happen sequence), Decision points and triggers, Communication cadence, 5) LEARN: Debrief framework (what to review after crisis resolves). Organize for immediate action clarity over perfection."

How to Use the Output:

- Execute stabilization actions immediately before complete assessment
- Time-box assessment phase don't get paralyzed seeking perfect information
- Use recommended option as starting point but apply your judgment and context
- Actually conduct the debrief after crisis learning prevents recurrence

Key Consideration: In crisis, decisive action with 80% information beats perfect analysis with 100% information that arrives too late. Move quickly but thoughtfully.

Part III: Leading Organizations - AI Tools for Organizational Leadership

TOOL 9: CULTURE ARCHITECTURE DESIGNER

Leadership Challenge: You're building or strengthening organizational culture using the Culture Architecture Model (Values→Behaviors→Systems→Stories).

AI Prompt:

"Help me design sustainable high-performance culture using the Culture Architecture Model. Our organization: [brief description]. Our stated values: [list 3-5 core values]. Current cultural reality: [what you observe be honest about gaps]. Create: 1) VALUES: For each value, specific behavioral definitions (observable actions that demonstrate it), Testing scenarios (situations where value would be challenged), 2) BEHAVIORS: Key behavior categories (how we treat each other, approach work, handle mistakes, communicate, develop others), Specific standards for each category, Peer accountability mechanisms, 3) SYSTEMS: Hiring/onboarding alignment with values, Performance management that reinforces culture, Recognition/rewards for cultural exemplars, Development investments, Decision-making processes, 4) STORIES: Types of stories we need (origin, values-in-action, cultural heroes, crisis response, learning/growth), Story collection and sharing practices. Be specific about what to implement, not just what to aspire to."

How to Use the Output:

- Start with values and behaviors make these crystal clear before building systems
- Audit existing systems against desired culture eliminate contradictions
- Begin telling cultural stories immediately don't wait for systems to be perfect
- Involve the team in culture building ownership comes from co-creation

Key Consideration: Culture is what you do when nobody's watching. Systems and stories matter, but leader modeling of values is the foundation.

TOOL 10: TEAM AI CAPABILITY BUILDER

Leadership Challenge: You want to build AI capability across your team to multiply organizational effectiveness.

AI Prompt:

"Help me build AI capability across my team. Team profile: Size: [number], Roles: [brief description], Current AI usage: [none/basic/varied], Technical sophistication: [low/medium/high], Key workflows: [major recurring tasks]. Create a 90-day AI integration program:

1) AWARENESS (Weeks 1-2): Introduction session content (what AI can/can't do, why it matters for our work), Demonstration of 3-5 relevant AI use cases specific to our work,

2) EXPERIMENTATION (Weeks 3-6): Specific AI tasks for team members to try (matched to their roles), Template prompts for common team workflows, Bi-weekly sharing sessions (what worked, what didn't),

3) ADOPTION (Weeks 7-10): Team AI workflow creation (systematic processes using AI), Peer coaching pairs (more experienced help less experienced),

4) OPTIMIZATION (Weeks 11-12): Team best practices documentation, Shared prompt library, Continuous improvement process. Include metrics to track adoption and impact."

How to Use the Output:

- Lead the AI adoption yourself model the behaviors you

want the team to develop

- Make experimentation psychologically safe celebrate learning from failures
- Share your own AI successes and failures to normalize the learning process
- Document team discoveries in real-time build institutional AI knowledge

Key Consideration: Team AI capability is competitive advantage. Organizations that build this systematically will outperform those where AI usage is random and individual.

How to Use This Toolkit Effectively

You now have ten powerful AI tools for leadership challenges. Here's how to maximize their value:

1. Start with Your Most Pressing Challenge

Don't try to use all ten tools immediately. Identify your most urgent leadership challenge right now and use the corresponding tool. Master one tool at a time rather than dabbling in many.

2. Customize Prompts to Your Context

These prompts are templates, not scripts. Add details about your specific situation, organization, constraints, and objectives. The more context you provide, the more relevant AI output becomes.

3. Iterate on Output

First AI response is rarely perfect. Ask follow-up questions, request refinements, or ask AI to approach from different angles. Iteration produces better results than single-shot prompts.

4. Apply Your Judgment

AI provides options and analysis you provide judgment. Don't follow AI recommendations blindly. Use them to inform your decisions, not replace your decision-making.

5. Document What Works

When you find an effective prompt or workflow, save it. Build your personal library of proven AI tools. Share effective tools with colleagues to multiply impact.

6. Combine Tools for Complex Challenges

Some leadership challenges require multiple tools. For instance, strategic change might need the Adaptability Planning tool, the Communication tool, and the Crisis Response tool. Don't feel limited to one tool per situation.

7. Share and Learn

When you discover improvements to these tools or create new ones, share them with your leadership community. Collective learning accelerates everyone's AI capability development.

Chapter Summary: Your AI Leadership Toolkit

This chapter provided ten practical AI tools aligned to the leadership frameworks throughout this book:

- Part I - Leading Yourself: Confidence building, self-awareness, communication preparation, adaptability planning

- Part II - Leading Others: Leadership transition, development plans, strategic anticipation, crisis response
- Part III - Leading Organizations: Culture building, team AI capability development

Each tool includes the prompt to use, how to use the output, and key considerations for effectiveness. These aren't theoretical approaches that work in real leadership situations.

The goal isn't to use AI for everything, it's to use AI strategically for the challenges where it creates the most value. Start with your most pressing challenge, master that tool, then expand to others as you build capability.

Gandhi taught that practice is worth more than preaching. You have the tools. Now use them. Don't just read about AI-enhanced leadership practice it. Start this week with one tool for one challenge. Your leadership effectiveness will multiply as you integrate these tools into your regular practice.

In Chapter 12, we'll complete the journey by exploring how to lead the AI-enabled organization creating systems, culture, and capabilities that sustain AI-enhanced performance at scale.

Tools are only valuable when used. Use these.

Chapter 12

Leading the AI-Enabled Organization

"The best way to predict the future is to create it."

Peter Drucker

The Organization That Multiplied Its Impact

Over my 40+ years of leadership from Director of Budget and Management through Chief Administrative Officer, six years as Chief of Staff to the Governor, leadership of Maryland's technology initiatives, and two decades building Great Foods LLC I've learned a fundamental truth: individual leader capability matters, but organizational capability matters more.

As Chair of Maryland's Information Technology Board, I saw this principle play out powerfully. We weren't just implementing technology, we were building systematic capability across state government to leverage technology for better service, efficiency, and decision-making. The organizations that succeeded weren't those with the best individual technical experts. They were the ones that built *organizational* technology capability systems, processes, culture, and collective competence that transcended any individual.

The same principle applies to AI. Individual leaders using AI to multiply their personal effectiveness is valuable. But organizations that systematically build AI capabilities that embed it into culture, operations, decision-making, and development will create sustainable competitive advantage that individual AI usage cannot match.

I've watched this evolution in my consulting work through Strategic Solutions Center. Clients who treat AI as individual productivity tools see modest improvements. Clients who build organizational AI capability see transformation faster strategic planning, better decision-making, more personalized customer service, accelerated innovation, and significantly higher performance across all dimensions.

One client organization provides a compelling example. When they started, AI usage was sporadic, a few tech-savvy individuals experimenting, but no systematic approach. We built organizational AI capability over 18 months: established governance and guidelines, created shared workflows and prompt libraries, trained leaders at all levels, integrated AI into strategic planning and operations, built culture that encouraged AI experimentation and learning.

The results were dramatic. Strategic planning cycles that previously took three months now took six weeks with better quality analysis. Customer service response time decreased 40%

while satisfaction increased. Leadership development scaled to reach five times as many people with more personalization. Innovation pipeline doubled as teams used AI to generate and evaluate more ideas faster.

But the most significant change was cultural. AI capability became organizational DNA something everyone knew how to leverage, not just technology specialists. New hires learned AI workflows as part of onboarding. Teams shared AI discoveries and built on each other's innovations. Leaders at all levels used AI to extend their impact.

This is what leading the AI-enabled organization means: Building systematic capability, not just individual competence. Creating culture and systems where AI amplifies everyone's effectiveness. Developing organizational capacity that compounds over time rather than depending on isolated champions.

What Makes an Organization AI-Enabled?

Peter Drucker taught us to create the future rather than just predict it. AI-enabled organizations are creating a different future one where human capability is systematically amplified by intelligent technology.

But what exactly makes an organization "AI-enabled" versus just "using AI occasionally"? Based on my experience helping organizations make this transition, AI-enabled organizations share five defining characteristics:

1. AI Capability Is Widespread, Not Concentrated

In traditional organizations, AI expertise concentrates in IT or data science teams. In AI-enabled organizations, AI capability exists throughout leaders at all levels, frontline employees, support functions. Everyone has baseline AI literacy and many have advanced AI skills relevant to their work. AI isn't something "the tech people do" it's something everyone leverages.

2. AI Integration Is Systematic, Not Sporadic

AI-enabled organizations embed AI into standard workflows and processes. Strategic planning systematically uses AI for scenario analysis. Decision-making processes incorporate AI-generated options. Development plans leverage AI for personalization at scale. Communication preparation routinely uses AI for drafting and refinement. This isn't experimental it's operational.

3. Learning About AI Is Continuous, Not One-Time

AI capabilities evolve rapidly. AI-enabled organizations

maintain continuous learning posture regular sharing of AI discoveries, systematic experimentation with new capabilities, active refinement of existing workflows, documented knowledge that scales organizational learning. This is Covey's Habit 7 (Sharpen the Saw) applied organizationally.

4. CULTURE ENCOURAGES AI EXPERIMENTATION, NOT JUST EFFICIENCY

Some organizations treat AI purely as efficiency tool do existing work faster. AI-enabled organizations also use AI for exploration what's newly possible? What couldn't we do before that we can do now? What customer needs could we address? What innovations could we pursue? Culture values AI-enabled innovation, not just AI-driven productivity.

5. LEADERSHIP MODELS AI PARTNERSHIP WHILE MAINTAINING HUMAN CENTRICITY

Leaders in AI-enabled organizations visibly use AI and share their learning. But they also maintain core human leadership genuine relationships, values-based decisions, investment in personal development, and authentic communication. AI amplifies their leadership; it doesn't replace it. They model the balance between AI capability and human centricity.

Framework: The AI-Enabled Organization Model

Building an AI-enabled organization requires systematic approach across multiple dimensions. I've developed what I call the AI-Enabled Organization Model a framework for creating organizational AI capability that sustains and compounds over time.

The model has four foundational pillars:

GOVERNANCE → CAPABILITY → INTEGRATION → EVOLUTION

Pillar 1: Governance - Establishing the Foundation

Governance creates the foundation for sustainable AI capability. Without clear governance, AI usage becomes chaotic some people racing ahead creating risk, others paralyzed by uncertainty, no organizational learning or standards.

Effective AI governance includes:

Clear Principles and Guidelines: What's encouraged? What's prohibited? What requires approval? These don't need to be comprehensive policies simple, clear principles work better than elaborate rule books.

Example principles: "Use AI to amplify human judgment, not replace it." "Always verify AI output for critical decisions." "Protect confidential information don't input sensitive data into public AI tools." "Share AI discoveries that could benefit colleagues." "Maintain authentic human connection in all stakeholder interactions."

Risk Management: Identify and address AI-related risks data privacy, bias, over-reliance, misinformation, competitive intelligence leakage. Create safeguards without creating bureaucracy.

Ethical Standards: How do your organizational values (from Chapter 9) apply to AI usage? If you value integrity, what does that mean for AI-generated content? If you value service, how does AI enhance rather than diminish service quality?

Decision Rights: Who decides what regarding AI? What's centralized (organization-wide tools, major investments)? What's decentralized (individual workflow choices, experimentation)? Clear decision rights prevent both chaos and bottlenecks.

Accountability: Who's responsible for AI capability development? Who ensures governance is followed? Who drives organizational AI learning? Accountability can't be diffused to "everyone" someone must own it.

Governance essentials:

- Start simple basic principles, not comprehensive policies
- Focus on enablement, not restriction governance should accelerate AI adoption safely
- Evolve governance as you learn don't lock into rigid rules prematurely
- Communicate governance clearly and repeatedly people can't follow what they don't know
- Lead by example senior leaders must visibly follow governance they establish

PILLAR 2: CAPABILITY - BUILDING ORGANIZATIONAL COMPETENCE

Governance establishes the rules; capability building creates the competence. This is systematic development of AI skills, knowledge, and confidence across the organization.

Capability building has several dimensions:

Baseline AI Literacy: Everyone in the organization should understand what AI can and can't do, how to use it responsibly, and basic prompt engineering. This isn't deep technical knowledge it's practical working knowledge.

Example: At one client organization, we created a 2-hour baseline training covering AI capabilities, limitations, responsible use, and 10 common use cases relevant to their work. Every employee completed this within their first month. This created shared language and baseline competence.

Role-Specific AI Skills: Different roles need different AI capabilities. Leaders need AI for strategic analysis and decision support. Developers need AI for code generation and debugging. Customer service needs AI for response quality. Sales needs AI for proposal development. Build role-specific capability, not just generic training.

Shared Workflow Library: Document effective AI workflows and prompts so people don't reinvent solutions. When someone discovers an excellent way to use AI for meeting preparation, capture it and share it. Build institutional knowledge.

Peer Learning: Create regular forums where people share AI discoveries, challenges, and solutions. Monthly AI learning sessions where team members demonstrate what they've learned. Peer learning scales faster and sticks better than formal training alone.

Expert Support: Identify AI champions with advanced capability who can coach others. Make their expertise available without creating bottlenecks. They're guides, not gatekeepers.

Practice Opportunities: From Chapter 1, we know competence comes from preparation. Create safe environments for AI practice sandbox projects, low-stakes experiments, protected learning time. People build capability through doing, not just learning.

Capability building essentials:

- Make AI capability development expected, not optional part of everyone's role
- Resource it appropriately allocate time and budget for learning
- Recognize and celebrate AI capability growth make it culturally valued
- Measure capability development track skills, usage, and impact
- Connect capability to performance people who develop AI skills should see career benefit

PILLAR 3: INTEGRATION - EMBEDDING AI INTO OPERATIONS

Capability without integration remains potential, not performance. Integration means embedding AI into how work actually gets done not as optional enhancement but as standard practice.

Integration happens across multiple operational dimensions:

Strategic Planning: From Chapter 7, strategic thinking drives anticipation and preparation. Integrate AI into planning cycles, scenario generation, implication analysis, option development, strategy communication. Make AI-enhanced planning the norm.

Decision-Making: Important decisions deserve thorough analysis. Integrate AI into decision processes rapid option generation, trade-off analysis, stakeholder impact mapping, decision documentation. Leaders still make final calls, but with AI-enhanced analysis.

Communication: From Chapter 3, communication quality drives performance. Integrate AI into communication workflows, message drafting, audience customization, clarity checking, follow-up documentation. Communication becomes faster and better simultaneously.

Development: From Chapter 6, development is core to leadership. Integrate AI into development systems personalized learning plans at scale, coaching question generation, progress tracking, feedback synthesis. Development reaches more people with higher quality.

Problem-Solving: When challenges arise, integrate AI into problem-solving approach root cause analysis, solution generation, implementation planning. Teams solve problems faster and more comprehensively.

Knowledge Management: Integrate AI into how knowledge is captured, organized, and accessed meeting documentation, process description, lessons learned, expertise preservation. Institutional knowledge compounds rather than evaporates.

Customer/Stakeholder Interaction: Integrate AI into stakeholder engagement needs analysis, personalized communication, rapid response, relationship documentation. Stakeholders experience better service without losing human connection.

Integration essentials:

- Start with high-impact, high-frequency workflows integrate where it matters most

- Make integration systematic, not random build it into standard processes
- Document integrated workflows so they're repeatable and trainable
- Monitor integration effectiveness measure time saved, quality improved, capabilities enabled
- Refine continuously integration should improve over time, not stagnate

PILLAR 4: EVOLUTION - CONTINUOUS ADVANCEMENT

AI technology evolves rapidly. Organizations that treat AI capability as static will fall behind. AI-enabled organizations build continuous evolution into their DNA constantly learning, experimenting, adapting, and advancing.

Evolution mechanisms include:

Systematic Experimentation: Allocate time and resources for AI experimentation. Give teams permission to test new AI capabilities, explore novel applications, and discover what's newly possible. Not everything will work, but experimentation drives breakthrough discoveries.

Learning Capture: When people discover effective AI applications or learn important lessons, capture and share that learning. Create repositories of AI best practices, failed experiments (so others don't repeat them), and emerging patterns.

Technology Monitoring: Assign someone to monitor AI technology evolution new capabilities, new tools, new applications in your industry. Bring discoveries back to the organization for evaluation and potential adoption.

Workflow Refinement: Regularly review and improve integrated AI workflows. What's working well? What's not delivering expected value? What could be better? Continuous refinement prevents stagnation.

Capability Advancement: As AI technology advances, organizational capability must advance. Periodic refresher training, exposure to new techniques, skill development for emerging capabilities. This is Covey's Habit 7 applied to AI continuously sharpen organizational AI capability.

Strategic Reassessment: AI creates new strategic possibilities. Regularly ask: What can we do now that we couldn't do before? What customers needs can we address? What competitive advantages can we create? Let AI capability inform strategy evolution.

Evolution essentials:

- Make evolution expected, not exceptional build it into normal rhythm
- Celebrate intelligent experiments that fail they drive learning
- Share learning broadly what one team discovers benefits everyone
- Resource evolution appropriately innovation requires investment
- Lead evolution from the top senior leaders must visibly champion advancement

Getting Started: Building Your AI-Enabled Organization

The AI-Enabled Organization Model shows what to build. But where do you start? Here's the roadmap I recommend based on helping multiple organizations make this transition:

PHASE 1: LEADERSHIP FOUNDATION (MONTHS 1-3)

Start at the top. Leadership must understand AI capability, use it personally, and commit to organizational AI enablement before cascading to the organization.

- Senior leaders develop personal AI capability (Chapters 10-11)
- Establish AI governance principles and decision rights
- Identify AI champions who will drive organizational capability building
- Define success metrics for AI enablement
- Create communication plan for AI enablement initiative

PHASE 2: CAPABILITY BUILDING (MONTHS 4-9)

Develop widespread AI capability through training, practice, and peer learning.

- Launch baseline AI literacy training for all employees
- Develop role-specific AI training and workflows
- Create shared workflow library and prompt repository
- Establish regular AI learning forums for sharing and peer coaching

- Run pilot projects integrating AI into high-value workflows

Phase 3: Integration (Months 10-15)

Embed AI into standard operations and processes across the organization.

- Integrate AI into strategic planning processes
- Build AI into decision-making frameworks
- Systematize AI use in communication, development, and problem-solving
- Document integrated workflows for repeatability
- Measure integration impact time saved, quality improved, new capabilities

Phase 4: Evolution and Optimization (Month 16+)

Build continuous improvement into organizational DNA.

- Establish systematic experimentation with emerging AI capabilities
- Refine workflows based on accumulated learning
- Advance organizational AI capability as technology evolves
- Explore strategic opportunities enabled by AI advancement
- Share organizational AI learning externally build reputation as AI-enabled leader

The Human-AI Partnership at Organizational Scale

Throughout this book, we've emphasized AI as amplifier, not replacement, for human leadership. This principle scales from individual to organization.

AI-enabled organizations don't become less human they become *more* human in the ways that matter. Here's how:

More Time for Human Connection: When AI handles analytical and administrative work, leaders have more time for genuine relationships coaching, mentoring, authentic communication, trust building. The principle of making people feel important and valued (core to my leadership) becomes more achievable at scale, not less.

Better Human Decisions: AI provides more comprehensive analysis faster, enabling better-informed human decisions. Decision quality improves because human judgment operates with superior information and broader options.

More Personalized Development: AI enables personalization at scale previously impossible. Development plans customized to individuals, coaching adapted to needs, learning resources matched to styles. People experience more personalized attention, not less.

Clearer Communication: AI helps clarify messages, customize for audiences, and ensure understanding. Communication becomes more effective and authentic simultaneously the CLEAR model from Chapter 3 enhanced by AI support.

Stronger Culture: From Chapter 9, culture requires values, behaviors, systems, and stories. AI doesn't replace culture it helps build and sustain it. AI can help identify cultural gaps, design reinforcing systems, and capture/share cultural stories at scale.

Greater Innovation: AI expands the realm of what's possible new services, new approaches, new solutions to old problems. Organizations become more innovative, not more mechanistic.

The key is intentional design. Without intention, AI could reduce human connection, create dependency, or undermine culture. With intention which is what the AI-Enabled Organization Model provides AI amplifies the best of human capability while handling work machines do better.

T.D. Jakes teaches that authenticity is essential for leadership. AI-enabled organizations remain authentic they're genuinely committed to people, values, and mission. AI is the tool that helps fulfill those commitments more effectively, not the purpose that replaces them.

Creating Your Future as an AI-Enabled Leader

Peter Drucker reminds us: "The best way to predict the future is to create it."

You now have everything you need to create your future as an AI-enabled leader:

- The leadership foundations (Chapters 1-4): Confidence, self-awareness, communication, adaptability

- The team leadership capabilities (Chapters 5-8): Transition from boss to leader, development, strategic thinking, crisis response
- The organizational leadership frameworks (Chapters 9-12): Culture building, AI as force multiplier, practical AI tools, AI-enabled organization model
- The timeless principles that transcend any technology: Service, excellence, development, integrity, anticipation, making people feel important

The choice now is yours. You can observe AI from the sidelines, waiting to see what happens. Or you can actively create your future by integrating AI into your leadership practice and building AI capability in your organization.

Based on four decades of leadership across county government, state administration, technology leadership, business building, and consulting, here's what I know:

Leadership has always been about multiplying impact developing people who develop others, building systems that outlast you, creating culture that transcends any individual. AI is simply the most powerful multiplication tool we've ever had access to.

The leaders who thrive won't be those with the most technical AI knowledge. They'll be those who maintain strong leadership fundamentals while strategically partnering with AI to amplify their impact.

The organizations that dominate won't be those that adopt AI first. They'll be those that build systematic AI capability governance, competence, integration, and evolution that compounds advantage over time.

And most importantly: AI-enabled leadership is still fundamentally about people. About making them feel valued and important. About developing their capabilities. About serving their growth. About maintaining integrity even under pressure. About building culture that brings out the best in everyone.

AI changes the tools. It doesn't change the purpose.

Your Next Steps: Starting Today

Don't wait for the "right time" to begin. Start today with these actions:

This Week:

- Choose one AI tool from Chapter 11 and use it for a real leadership challenge
- Share what you learn with at least one colleague
- Identify one leadership framework from this book to implement immediately

This Month:

- Develop your personal AI capability using the roadmap from Chapter 10
- Create your first AI workflow for a recurring leadership task
- Start one leadership development initiative using frameworks from Part I or II

This Quarter:

- Begin building team AI capability using guidance from this chapter
- Establish AI governance principles for your organization
- Measure the impact of AI integration on your leadership effectiveness

This Year:

- Build organizational AI capability across all four pillars (Governance, Capability, Integration, Evolution)
- Strengthen culture using the Culture Architecture Model from Chapter 9
- Multiply your impact by developing leaders who develop others

Final Words: Your Leadership Legacy

Leadership is measured not by what you accomplish during your tenure, but by what continues after you leave.

When I left my role as Chief of Staff after six years the longest tenure in Maryland history I could have measured success by the policies implemented or the crises navigated. But the measure that mattered most was what my colleague told me five years later: the culture we built together still thrived, the people we developed continued leading, and the standards we established persisted.

That's sustainable leadership. That's the goal.

AI gives you unprecedented capability to build this kind of lasting impact:

- Develop more people more deeply than ever before
- Build culture and systems that outlast you
- Document and transfer knowledge that prevents organizational amnesia
- Create capability that compounds as people develop people who develop people
- Scale the principle of making people feel important and valued to everyone you touch

But technology is just the amplifier. Your values, your commitment to people, your integrity, your service orientation these remain the foundation.

Les Brown teaches that it's not over until you win. Your leadership journey isn't over. You're not finished growing, learning, developing, or making impact. AI just expanded what's possible.

Stephen Covey's Seven Habits remain as relevant in the AI era as ever. Begin with the end in mind. Put first things first. Seek first to understand. Think win-win. Synergize. Sharpen the saw. Private victories still precede public victories.

T.D. Jakes reminds us that resilience bouncing forward, not just back is essential. AI capability is part of bouncing forward. It's how you emerge from challenges stronger than before.

I began this book sharing my journey 40+ years from county budget director through state leadership to business builder to consultant. The constant through every phase hasn't been specific techniques or technologies. It's been commitment to principles: service, excellence, development, integrity, anticipation, making people feel valued.

AI doesn't change those principles. It enables you to live them more fully, at greater scale, with deeper impact.

Your leadership matters. The people you develop matter. The culture you build matters. The legacy you leave matters.

Now you have the tools to multiply that impact beyond what any previous generation of leaders could achieve.

Use them wisely. Use them well. Use them in service of something bigger than yourself.

The future belongs to leaders who multiply their impact through intelligent partnerships with AI, with people, with purpose.

Go create that future.

Major F. Riddick, Jr.

About the Author

Major F. Riddick, Jr. brings more than 40 years of transformative leadership experience across public service, technology innovation, business building, and strategic consulting. His career exemplifies the principle that great leaders multiply their impact by developing others, building sustainable systems, and creating culture that outlasts any individual.

Public Service Leadership

Major's public service career includes serving as Director of Budget and Management and Chief Administrative Officer for county government, where he led organizational transformation and fiscal excellence. He then served six years as Chief of Staff to Maryland Governor Parris Glendening the longest-serving Chief of Staff in Maryland history. In this role, he orchestrated strategic initiatives, managed complex stakeholder relationships, and built high-performance teams that continued to excel long after his tenure.

Technology Innovation

As Chair of Maryland's Information Technology Board from 1995 to 2003, Major led the state's technology transformation, building systematic capability across government agencies to leverage technology for improved service delivery, efficiency, and decision-making. His leadership demonstrated that successful technology adoption requires organizational capability building, not just technical implementation a principle that drives his approach to AI integration today.

Business Leadership

Major founded and led Great Foods LLC for 20 years (2004-2024), building a successful airport concessions business in one of the most competitive industries. The company thrived through the 2008 financial crisis and multiple industry disruptions by maintaining strong culture, developing people at all levels, and adapting strategically to changing market conditions. His leadership created an organization where excellence, service, and people development were more than values they were daily practice.

Strategic Consulting

Through Strategic Solutions Center, Major helps organizations navigate complex challenges by integrating proven leadership principles with cutting-edge AI capabilities. He works with leaders to build sustainable high-performance cultures, develop systematic organizational capabilities, and multiply their impact through strategic AI partnerships. His consulting practice combines four decades of hands-on leadership experience with practical AI implementation expertise.

Leadership Philosophy

Major's leadership philosophy centers on five core values that have guided him throughout his career: Service (leadership is about serving others, not being served), Excellence (good enough isn't; strive for exceptional), Development (invest continuously in growing people's capabilities), Integrity (do what's right, especially when difficult), and Anticipation (think ahead, prepare proactively, position strategically). These timeless principles remain constant even as leadership tools evolve.

He is particularly known for the principle that "once you work for Major, you always work for Major" reflecting his deep commitment to developing leaders who go on to develop others, creating compounding impact across organizations and careers.

Current Focus

Today, Major focuses on helping leaders integrate AI capabilities while maintaining the human elements that make leadership effective genuine relationships, values-based decision-making, personal development, and authentic communication. He teaches that AI is a force multiplier for leadership, amplifying impact while never replacing the judgment, wisdom, and human connection that only people can provide.

Education

Major holds a Bachelor of Arts in Political Science and a Master of Arts in Public Administration and Urban Affairs from Virginia Tech, Blacksburg, Virginia. He also completed the Executive Leadership Program at the John F. Kennedy School of Government, Harvard University.

Connect with Major:

Website: www.strategicsolutionscenter.com

Email: mriddick@strategicsolutionscenter.com

LinkedIn: Major F. Riddick, Jr.

Made in the USA
Monee, IL
05 November 2026

67809044R00148